BUSINESS, TECHNOLOGY AND FINANCE

LONG TERM INTEREST RATES

DECLINES, DRIVERS, CONSIDERATIONS

BUSINESS, TECHNOLOGY AND FINANCE

Additional books in this series can be found on Nova's website under the Series tab.

Additional e-books in this series can be found on Nova's website under the e-book tab.

BUSINESS, TECHNOLOGY AND FINANCE

LONG TERM INTEREST RATES

DECLINES, DRIVERS, CONSIDERATIONS

DARYL WATKINS
EDITOR

NOVINKA

New York

Additional color graphics may be available in the e-book version of this book.

Library of Congress Cataloging-in-Publication Data

ISBN: 978-1-63483-747-7

Published by Nova Science Publishers, Inc. † New York

CONTENTS

PREFACE

The long-term interest rate is a central variable in the macroeconomy. It matters to borrowers looking to start a business or purchase a home; to lenders weighing the risks and rewards of extending credit; to savers preparing for college or retirement; and to policymakers gauging the state of the economy and financing government expenditure. The global financial crisis and the aggressive policy response pushed long-term interest rates in the United States and in many advanced economies to historically low levels. But today's low-rate environment is not just a cyclical story. Interest rates had been falling worldwide for nearly twenty years before the crisis. Despite the magnitude and persistence of the secular downtrend, the explanation for the decline is one of the most vexing questions faced by macroeconomists today. The future path of interest rates is even less clear. This book surveys the recent thinking on the many drivers of long-term interest rates in recent decades and going forward. In addition, this book provides a speech by Federal Reserve Board Governor Bernanke at the Sandridge Lecture which discusses the global saving glut and the U.S. current deficit.

In: Long Term Interest Rates
Editor: Daryl Watkins

ISBN: 978-1-63483-747-7

Chapter 1

LONG-TERM INTEREST RATES: A SURVEY*

Council of Economic Advisors

EXECUTIVE SUMMARY

The long-term interest rate is a central variable in the macroeconomy. It matters to borrowers looking to start a business or purchase a home; to lenders weighing the risks and rewards of extending credit; to savers preparing for college or retirement; and to policymakers gauging the state of the economy and financing government expenditure.

The global financial crisis and the aggressive policy response pushed long-term interest rates in the United States and in many advanced economies to historically low levels. But today's low- rate environment is not just a cyclical story. Interest rates had been falling worldwide for nearly twenty years before the crisis. Despite the magnitude and persistence of the secular downtrend, the explanation for the decline is one of the most vexing questions faced by macroeconomists today. The future path of interest rates is even less clear.

This report surveys the recent thinking on the many drivers of long-term interest rates in recent decades and going forward. It concludes:

---

* This is an edited, reformatted and augmented version of a report issued by the Executive Office of the President, July 2015.

- **The decline in long-term interest rates over the past thirty years was real, global, and unexpected.** While lower inflation explains some of the decline in nominal interest rates, the downtrend is evident even when adjusting nominal interest rates for the rate of inflation. The decline has also been evident across a wide range of countries, reflecting the increasing integration of the global economy. Financial markets and professional forecasters alike consistently failed to predict the secular shift, focusing too much on cyclical factors and missing the long-term trend.
- **The decline is consistent with several theoretical frameworks economists have used to analyze interest rates.** The interest rate settles at the level that equates the supply of saving with the demand for investment, and innumerable factors affect both sides of the equation. Many frameworks suggest that long-term interest rates are closely related to productivity growth. Other factors such as the rate of population growth and technological advance, as well as aggregate demand and the stance of fiscal and monetary policy, also play a role.
- **A number of factors, both transitory and longer-lived, have contributed to the decline— with many of these factors suggesting that long-run equilibrium interest rates have fallen.** Transitory factors include global fiscal and monetary policies, shifts in the term premium and inflation risk, and post-crisis private-sector deleveraging. More persistent factors include lower potential output and productivity growth, shifting demographics, and the global "saving glut."

Ultimately, interest rates reflect underlying macroeconomic conditions; there is no "optimal" long-term rate of interest. Rather, policy should support long-run growth, maintain price stability, and support a stable financial system.

I. Introduction

The long-term interest rate is a central variable in the macroeconomy. A change in the long-term interest rate affects the value of accumulated savings, the cost of borrowing, the valuation of investment projects, and the sustainability of fiscal deficits. A projection of the long-term interest rate is therefore a key input to the Administration forecast underlying the President's budget.

Interest rates at all maturities have declined over the past thirty years. At least some of the decline is due to cyclical factors that will likely diminish as the economy recovers further from the Great Recession and economic policies normalize. But many have speculated that even after policy normalizes, the underlying long-term interest rate will remain lower than it had been historically. This Report investigates this question, examining the key determinants of long-term interest rates—with a particular focus on the factors that seem most important in determining the rate on the 10-year Treasury note ten years from now.

The nominal interest rate is most usefully conceptualized as the sum of the *real* interest rate and the expected rate of inflation (Fisher 1930). The equilibrium real interest rate is the rate at which the supply of saving is equal to the demand for investment, and it equates the marginal return on investment to the compensation savers earn for delaying consumption. Ultimately, nominal interest rates are jointly determined by a host of factors including expectations about the rates of economic growth and inflation, the cyclical position of the economy, the volatility of financial markets, and consumer preferences for smoothing consumption and absorbing risk. As markets have become more integrated internationally, conditions in foreign markets play an increasingly central role in determining interest rates in the United States, especially long-term rates.

Section II reviews trends in real and nominal interest rates and inflation. Since the early 1980s, both nominal and real long-term interest rates have declined. Currently, the nominal interest rate on the 10-year Treasury note hovers above 2 percent, and the average comparable interest rate for some of the other G7 countries is below one percent. Even at today's low inflation rates, the *ex post* real interest rate (the nominal rate less realized inflation) on long-term bonds has dipped into negative territory for some advanced countries.

Section III draws on economic theory for a framework to think about real and nominal interest rates in general equilibrium and at different horizons. A basic growth model generates a fundamental relationship between real per capita consumption growth, the underlying rate of growth in the economy, and the real interest rate, according to which higher growth implies a higher real interest rate. This relationship is useful for explaining real interest rates in the absence of uncertainty about future economic conditions, but misses the role of risk in influencing real as well as nominal interest rates. Financial models are useful for thinking about such risks, and how these complicate the simple Fisher relationship between real and nominal interest rates for longer maturity bonds, though they are less successful at linking rates of return to long-run economic fundamentals empirically. Both of these approaches are used to evaluate historical and more recent data on long-term interest rates. The section also discusses application of these insights in economies that are integrated with world markets.

Section IV returns to the question of why long-term interest rates are currently so low and the implications of low rates today for future long-term rates. The potential explanations are high global saving, demographic changes, low productivity growth, and falling term premiums connected with the aftermath of the global financial crisis. An important question, closely related to the global saving glut and secular stagnation hypotheses, is the extent to which these low interest rates will persist. There is no definitive answer to the question, but many hypotheses point to the possibility that while long-term real and nominal interest rates will likely rise off their current lows, their long-run levels have fallen relative to those that prevailed before the financial crisis.

The drivers of long-term interest rates are complex and the report delves into these issues in some detail. To assist readers less interested in the technical details, lists of key take-aways conclude section II, sections IIIa, b, and c, and section IV.

II. Some Observations on Long-Term Interest Rates

Interest Rates Have Declined Over the Last Thirty Years

Figure 1 provides a long-run perspective on U.S. nominal interest rates, plotting the annual yields on one- and 10-year Treasury notes since 1871.[1] The figure highlights successive eras in economic history (e.g., the gold standard era and the Bretton Woods era). Several things stand out in the figure. First, nominal interest rates follow long swings and can spend extensive periods of time away from their long-run historical averages. Second, both the 10- and the one-year nominal interest rates have declined fairly steadily from their highs in the early 1980s. A third observation is that since the onset of the Great Depression during the interwar period, the 10-year rate has tended to be—though is not always—above the one-year rate. The relatively higher 10-year rate reflects the compensation investors require for holding a longer-term asset. The 10-year rate also tends to be less volatile than the one-year rate because the 10-year rate reflects an average of expected future short-term rates, as discussed below, and averaging smooths much of the year- to-year fluctuation in the shorter rate. Finally, the figure shows that since 2010, the one-year nominal interest rate has been below 0.46 percent—a level not observed previously in these data, though from 1935-45, the rate hovered between 0.5 and 1.0 percent.

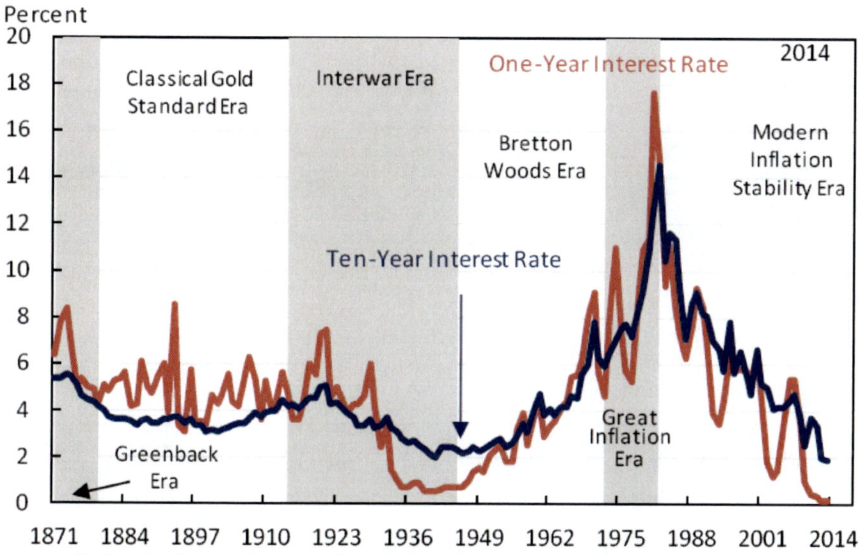

Source: Robert J. Shiller (Yale University);Federal Reserve Board.

Figure 1. One-Year and 10-YearU.S. Nominal Interest Rates.

Figure 2 plots the real interest rate on the 10-year Treasury note, where the real interest rate is proxied by the difference between the nominal annual yield on the 10-year note less the five-year unweighted moving average of current and past annual inflation.[2] The real interest rate is the rate that influences economic activity—ultimately, market participants care about the returns to their saving and investment decisions net of inflation.[3] The behavior of the real interest rate varies across monetary regimes, exhibiting less volatility during the latter part of the Bretton Woods era, when the dollar's exchange rates to foreign currencies were pegged and inflation relatively stable, and during the modern inflation-stability period since the mid-1980s. Like the nominal interest rates in Figure 1, the real 10-year interest rate has been on a steady decline since the mid-1980s, undergoing the longest sustained decline since 1876. However, the decline in the real rate is also a longer-run phenomenon. A trend line fitted to the data in Figure 2 shows that the real 10-year rate has declined slightly under 2 basis points per year on average between 1876 and 2013, though the fit of the trend line is weak.[4]

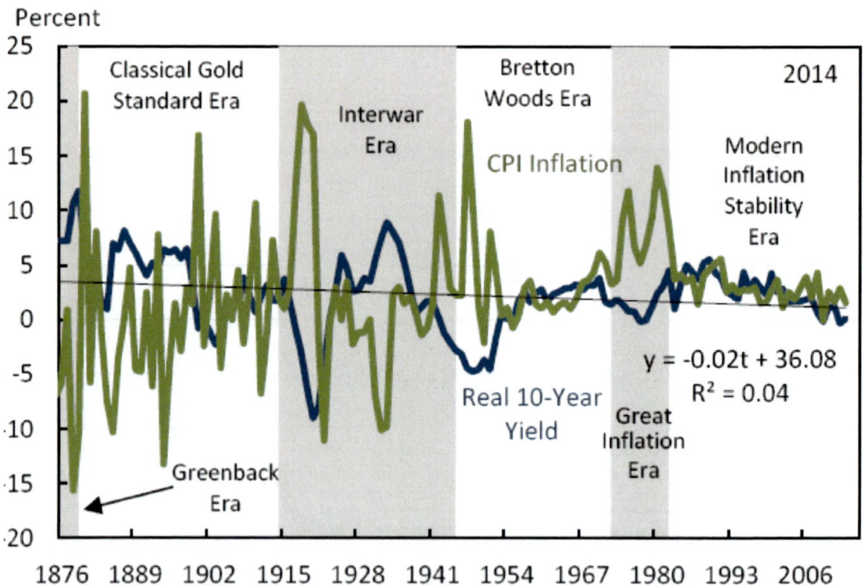

Source: Robert J. Shiller (Yale University)

Figure 2. Real Interest Rate on the 10-Year Treasury and Inflation.

The real interest rate has recently dipped into negative territory. Negative real interest rates have been observed previously in U.S. history and indeed have been much more negative—reaching almost negative 10 percent in the aftermath of World War I and negative 5 percent after World War II. In those episodes, the exceptionally negative real rate was a consequence of very high inflation. At the current time, it is the low nominal interest rate and not high inflation that is behind a negative real interest rate.

Along with the nominal 10-year rate (in blue) from 1980 on, Figure 3 shows the real interest rate as measured in Figure 2 (in red) along with two additional proxy measures. The purple line is the interest rate on TIPS (the return on the 10-year Treasury note indexed to the consumer price index, or CPI), available only since 1997 when the security was first issued. In addition, the annual nominal yield less expected 10-year inflation as reported by the

Survey of Professional Forecasters is shown in green.[5] Relatively low variance of inflation after the early 1980s has made inflation expectations more stable. Therefore, the real interest rate is highly correlated with the nominal interest rate. The two additional measures of the real interest rate shown in Figure 3 display the same declining path noted in Figure 2.

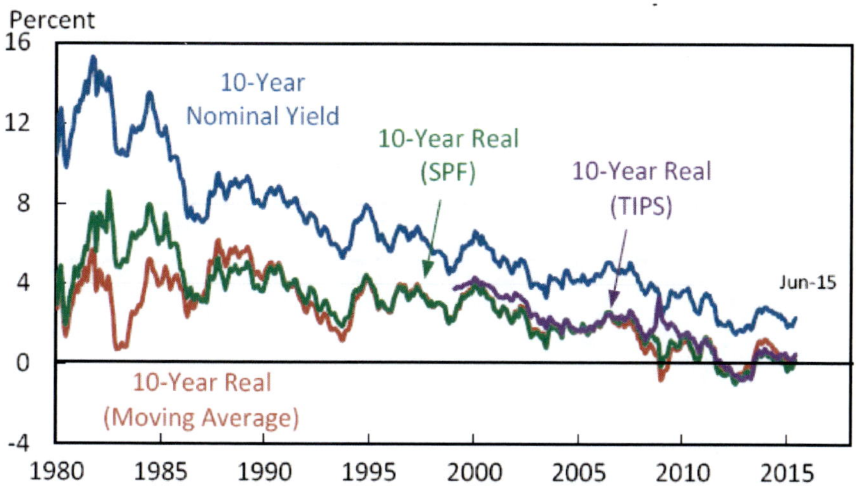

Note: 10-Year Real (Moving Average) rates are nominal Treasury yields adjusted for 5-year lagged moving average of CPI inflation. 10-Year Real (TIPS) rates are yields on Treasury Inflation-Protected Securities. 10-Year Real (SPF) rates are nominal 10-year Treasury yields adjusted using median 10- year CPI inflation expectations.

Source: Federal Reserve Board; Federal Reserve Bank of Philadelphia, Survey of Professional Forecasters.

Figure 3. 10-YearNominal and Real U.S. Treasury RatesPercent.

For forecasting and for understanding the macroeconomy, it is important to grasp the causes and likely persistence of the decline in long-term interest rates over the past three decades. Section IV will discuss several hypotheses in detail, but one important piece of evidence is that interest rates have declined not only in the United States, but also in a wide range of countries across the world.

Declining Long-Term Interest Rates are a Global Phenomenon

Figure 4 shows the steady decline in long-term nominal rates for a sample of OECD economies. Japan's long-term nominal rate is notably lower than the rest over most of the period shown and the fall in its rate over time less sharp, but other countries' rates have moved closer to Japan's levels in recent years. Real long-term interest rates have fallen as well. Nominal interest rates on 10-year bonds currently fall short of inflation in Japan, France, Canada, Sweden, and Denmark.[6]

In Section IIIc, we discuss the role of global factors in determining interest rates.

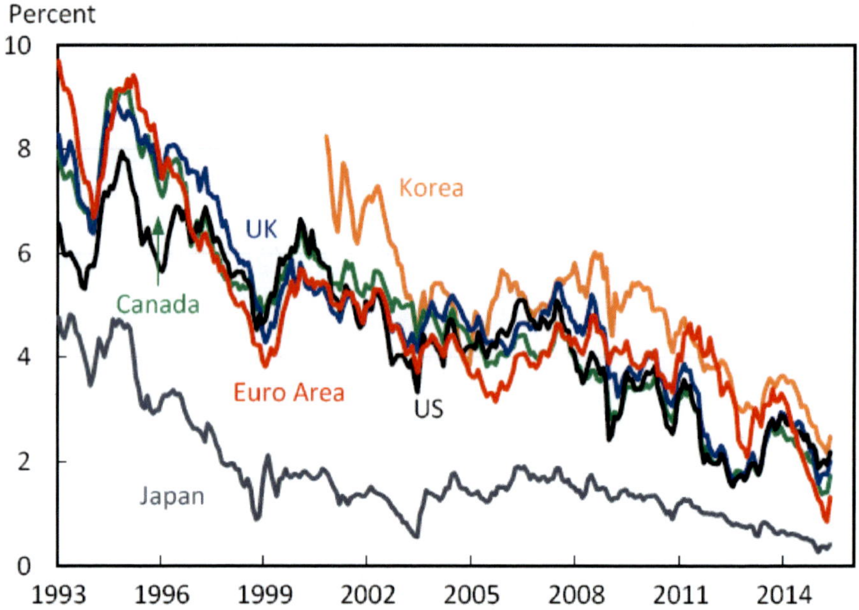

Source: National Sources.

Figure 4. Nominal 10-Year Yields.

Forecasts Have Largely Missed the Decline in Long-Term Interest Rates

Past forecasts have largely missed the decline in long-term interest rates. This can be seen in Figure 5, which shows past private-sector forecasts along with the actual path of nominal 10-year Treasury rates since 1995.[7] Although economists' forecasts steadily declined after 1995, their pace of decline has lagged well behind the realized drop-off in interest rates. Indeed, since 1996, long-range private sector forecasts have exhibited a root mean square error of 2.7 percentage points relative to the nominal Treasury rate realized 10 years later.[8] The Administration's latest forecast for the nominal 10-year interest rate in 2025 is 4.4 percent, in line with the levels forecast by private-sector economists. The long-run forecast of 2.0 percent personal consumption expenditure (PCE) price-index inflation (the Federal Reserve's inflation target) implies an expected long-run long-term real interest rate of 2.4 percent for 2025.

Of course, it is difficult to make predictions about the very long run because so many conditions can change over that time horizon. However, even at shorter horizons, interest rate forecasts have tended to be inaccurate. Between 1984 and 2012, CBO, private-sector forecasters, and the Administration all systematically overestimated the path of nominal interest rates just two years into the future (CBO 2015a).

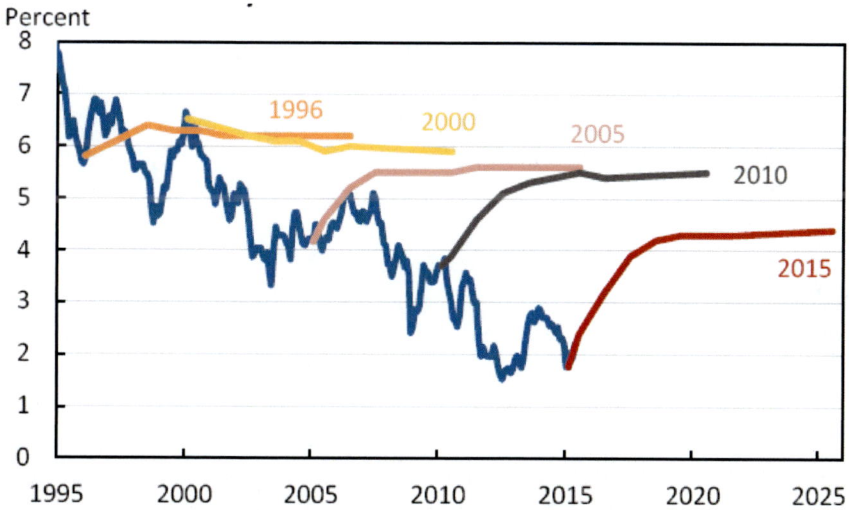

Note: Forecasts are those reported by Blue Chip Economic Indicators released in March of the given calendar year, the median of over 50 private-sector economists.
Source: Blue Chip Economic Indicators, Aspen Publishers.

Figure 5. 10-Year Treasury Rates and Historical Economist Forecasts.

A central question in forming a long-run forecast is whether interest rates are statistically stationary—i.e., whether they have a tendency to return to a definite long-run mean value or average. To the extent interest rates are mean-reverting, the historical average may contain the most useful information for projecting the long-run long-term interest rate. On the other hand, if changes in interest rates are permanent (or at least, highly persistent), recent data may contain more useful information about long-run interest rates than historical data. In general, econometric tests suggest that real and nominal interest rates revert to their mean very slowly, with close to unit root (non-stationary)[9] properties.[10] Tests for non-stationarity tend to be weak, however, in that distinguishing between a true unit root and mean reversion with very high persistence is difficult in a finite sample of data (Neely and Rapach 2008).

Economic theory strongly suggests that real interest rates are bounded, if not fully mean reverting (as discussed in more detail in section III).[11] A high return on investment should trigger a reallocation of resources from consumption toward capital accumulation, driving down the marginal product of capital and the real interest rate over time. Similarly, a low return on investment should induce consumers to increase current consumption and reduce capital investment, eventually driving up the real interest rate. Such economic forces should limit extremely high or extremely low real interest rates and work to push the rate back to intermediate levels. Indeed, were real interest rates to be literally non-stationary, the level of the real rate would pierce any upper or lower bound in finite time with a probability of one, an implication that is economically implausible and clearly not supported by the historical record.

In the current era of inflation targeting, inflation rates have tended to be moderate and stable, so the previous reasoning will by and large apply to the properties of nominal as well as real rates of interest. As noted above, however, interest rates do exhibit a high degree of persistence, raising the question of the underlying economic causes of long-run changes in interest rates and the forces that may be slowing their adjustment over time. We return to the specific question of why long-term interest rates are currently so low, and the implications for long-run equilibrium rates, in Section IV.

The data in Figure 5 suggest that past forecasts of long-term nominal interest rates have tended to err on the side of mean reversion. The long-run forecasts (the ends of the extended lines) lie within a fairly tight range of 4.4 to 6 percent, despite the fact that the nominal 10-year rate has swung from a low below 2 percent to a high of nearly 8 percent. The forecast range is consistent with the historical mean of the nominal long-term interest rate but may not accurately reflect possible changes in structural features of the economy. In light of the persisting downward trend in long-term interest rates, forecasters have incrementally lowered their expectations for the 10- year rate over the past two years, with the Administration forecast down by 60 basis points, the private-sector consensus forecast down by 30 basis points, and the CBO forecast down by 60 basis points.

Key Takeaways

- Real and nominal interest rates in the United States have been on a steady decline since the mid-1980s.
- Declining interest rates are a global phenomenon.
- It is difficult to forecast interest rates and forecasters largely missed the secular decline of the last three decades.

III. Interest Rates through the Lens of Economic Theory

A large number of factors play a role in determining interest rates and economic theory helps to provide a framework for sifting through them. A useful starting place for thinking about interest rates is the seminal work of Irving Fisher (1930), who characterized the equilibrium relationship between the nominal rate of return on an asset, the rate of inflation, and the compensation to savers for postponing consumption. Modern financial theory extends this core insight to environments with uncertainty by showing that any financial asset can be priced using a stochastic discount factor (SDF)—the rate at which savers trade off consumption today for future uncertain consumption. In general, the expected return on an asset depends on how long the asset holder must wait for the payoff, the asset holder's impatience (i.e., his or her desire to consume sooner rather than later), the asset holder's willingness to tolerate risk, properties of the asset holder's overall wealth portfolio, and the extent to which the asset being priced adds or reduces risk in the asset holder's portfolio.

In Section IIIa, we begin with a simple version of the Ramsey (1928) dynamic saving model that abstracts from uncertainty and generates a relatively simple relationship between the growth rate of per capita consumption and the real interest rate. Along the steady-state growth path, the growth rate of per capita consumption must be equal to the long-run growth rate of per capita output. When augmented with a forecast for the long-run rate of inflation, the Ramsey- model prediction therefore implies a forecast for the long-run nominal interest rate.

Section IIIb extends this framework to incorporate the effects of uncertainty about productivity and inflation. This permits a decomposition of the long-term nominal yield on a bond into three components: the expected path of the real short-term real interest rate, the expected rate of inflation, and the term premium (the compensation to the investor for holding a long-term bond and bearing the risk of fluctuations in its price). Each of the components is discussed in detail and related to evidence from financial markets. In the end, the macro model based on long-run growth, adjusted for expected inflation, generates an interest rate forecast that is in the same general range as estimates from the financial models that incorporate risk. This is not too surprising, as the underlying linkage between economic growth and interest rates ought to remain important even when there is long-term risk.

The discussion in sections IIIa and IIIb proceeds as if the United States were a closed economy, abstracting from the effects of international trade and capital flows. As barriers to international trade and capital mobility have come down, however, global factors have become increasingly important in the determination of U.S. interest rates. In Section IIIc, we discuss how the economic framework can be extended when countries are open to iternational trade and financial transactions.

III.a. Link between Economic Growth and the Real Interest Rate

The Ramsey model generates a fundamental link between per capita consumption growth, the real interest rate, and the growth rate of the economy. The model is based on the dynamic saving and investment decisions of a hypothetical, infinitely-lived representative household. (Appendix A provides a full characterization of the model and its solution.) In this setup, the household chooses an optimal saving/investment plan to maximize the present value of utility from current and future consumption. We begin with the simplest version of the model, which assumes that the household has perfect foresight about the future. Later discussion will take uncertainty into account.

The intertemporal optimality conditions for a household's preferred consumption and investment plan yield the standard Euler condition:

$$u'(c_t) = \beta u'(c_{t+1})(1 + r_{t+1}) \qquad (1)$$

Here, r_{t+1} indicates interest earned on savings between dates *t* and *t*+1 and c_t is consumption per worker on date *t*. The function *u*(*c*) measures the private value, or utility, that the consumer derives from consuming at rate *c* and *β* is the rate at which the consumer discounts next period's utility relative to today's. The left-hand-side of (1) is the opportunity cost of forgoing consumption (i.e., of saving) in period *t*. The right-hand-side shows the return to saving—the gross interest rate multiplied by the discounted marginal utility of future consumption. In equilibrium, the household will save up to the point where the gross return to saving is equal to the household's intertemporal marginal rate of substitution, $u'(c_t)/\beta u'(c_{t+1})$, this being the gross rate at which it is willing to sacrifice present consumption for future consumption.

Under standard functional forms for household preferences, the real interest rate can be written as a function of the growth rate of consumption per capita,

$$r_{t+1} = \rho + g_{t+1} \qquad (2)$$

where $g_{t+1} = ln(c_{t+1}) - ln(c_t)$, *ln* denotes the natural logarithm, and $\rho = 1/(1-\beta)$. The equilibrium real interest rate is increasing in per capita consumption growth and the subjective rate of discount (*ρ*), and is decreasing in the intertemporal elasticity of substitution (1/*σ*). Note that condition (2) holds between any two dates, and so will govern saving and investment decisions in both the short and the long runs. What is the significance of the two key parameters *ρ* and *σ*?

The discount rate *ρ* measures how much people value current consumption relative to future consumption. The more heavily households discount future consumption (the higher is *ρ* and the lower is *β*), the higher the rate of compensation the household will require for waiting to consume, and the higher, therefore, will be the real rate of interest. The discount rate is independent of the level of consumption and therefore enters equation (2) additively.

Estimates of the discount rate *ρ* vary widely depending on the data used and the empirical methodology (Frederick et al. 2002). Some studies calculate the discount rate implied by real-life microeconomic decisions that involve an intertemporal tradeoff, such as the decision to take a lump-sum retirement payment versus a stream of payments, or the decision to buy an energy-efficient air conditioner that will reduce electricity bills over the long run. Estimates of ρ from this approach range from a low of 1 percent per year to values over 200 percent (Moore and Viscusi 1990; Ruderman et al. 1987). Meanwhile, macro studies that draw on saving and consumption data obtain estimates ranging from 4 to 14 percent (Lawrance 1991; Carroll and Samwick 1997; Gourinchas and Parker 2002). These high implicit discount rates are hard to reconcile with prevailing low market interest rates: if individuals were truly so impatient, why should such a low interest rate clear the credit market? Many economists believe that estimates of ρ based on aggregate data and surveys overstate the extent to which people truly discount the value of future consumption. One problem is that there may be a time inconsistency in preferences—that is, one's subjective view of future consumption evaluated from today's vantage point may be different from the way one's "future self" will evaluate consumption tomorrow. Another issue is that it is difficult to isolate the impact of future unknowns, such as inflation, or other shocks to wealth, on future consumption, to obtain a "pure" measure of the trade-off between consumption today and consumption tomorrow.

The intertemporal elasticity of substitution, $1/\sigma$, measures the extent to which households are willing to give up consumption today for consumption tomorrow, taking into account diminishing marginal utility. If growth is expected to be high, people will try to borrow against their future higher income to consume more now, and this will drive up the interest rate. At some point, the higher interest rate will discourage borrowing and restore equilibrium between the return on capital investment (which reflects the ability to produce income in the future) and the household's desire to consume now. The interest-rate response depends on the interaction between σ and the growth rate of per capita consumption. If σ is less than 1 (and therefore the intertemporal elasticity of substitution is large), people are relatively willing to accommodate changes in the timing of consumption and do not require a high interest rate as compensation. If people are more resistant to shifting consumption across time ($\sigma > 1$ and the intertemporal elasticity of substitution is low), then the interest rate will react more strongly to changes in the growth rate of consumption.

There is even more debate about the value of σ than about the value of ρ. Because the elasticity interacts with the rate of consumption growth, the estimated relationship depends critically on what type of consumption and what interest rate one uses in the analysis. Estimated values of σ tend to be low when based on consumption data at the micro level (e.g., studies based on individual consumption choices), suggesting that people are fairly willing to substitute over time. Macroeconomic evidence on aggregate consumption growth—which tends to be fairly smooth— suggests values of σ around 1. Extremely high values of σ (low intertemporal elasticities of substitution) are needed to reconcile returns on financial assets, which tend to be highly volatile, with changes in aggregate consumption.[12]

Consumption Growth and the Real Interest Rate

Rose (1988) observed that if equation (2) is correct, interest rates and consumption growth should have similar statistical integration (or persistence) properties. Statistical tests confirm that that consumption growth rates are strongly mean reverting. Real interest rates exhibit much more persistence than consumption growth, however, revert to mean only at a very slow rate, as noted earlier.[13] The mismatch between the statistical properties of consumption growth and real interest rates suggests that there are shocks that cause the two series to deviate, and the deviation can persist for long periods of time. For example, persistent changes in the discount rate ρ could be one such factor. Demographic factors, to be discussed below, could also play a role in weakening the link in the data between aggregate consumption growth and interest rates.

Not surprisingly, empirical studies find that growth rates in per capita consumption do a poor job of predicting out-of-sample real interest rates and vice versa.

Productivity Growth and the Real Interest Rate

In the Ramsey model's equilibrium, the interest on saving is equal to the marginal return on capital investment. Capital is combined with labor to produce a good that can be consumed or invested. Growth in the economy is driven by labor-augmenting technological progress (at rate g) and population growth (at rate n). Population growth expands the raw number of workers, while technological advance expands the number of "effective" workers by making each one more productive over time. Along a balanced growth path with a constant level of capital per effective unit of labor, the productive efficiency of each unit of labor grows at rate g and total output and consumption at rate $n + g$. (For simplicity, the discussion abstracts from depreciation of capital.) Note that the rate of population growth does not affect the balanced growth path's steady-state interest rate because along that path, the household saves just enough for future generations to keep the ratio of capital per unit of effective labor constant. The rate of productivity growth, g, determines the growth rate of output per person and consumption per person.

Under the assumption that preferences are stable and that household consumption reflects productivity developments, the model suggests that periods of high per capita consumption growth should coincide with high labor productivity growth and high real interest rates. Figure 6 shows average four-quarter growth in output per hour, per capita real consumption (as measured by PCE), and the real interest rate since 1958. The series are smoothed to highlight the medium- to long-run patterns in the data. The paths for consumption growth and the real interest rate are correlated throughout the sample. The link between the real interest rate and labor productivity growth is still apparent but less strong than the link with consumption growth. This discrepancy arises because per capita consumption growth is predicted to exactly track labor productivity growth only in a hypothetical balanced-growth equilibrium, whereas over briefer time spans measured labor productivity growth is likely to be imperfectly correlated with current and expected future incomes.

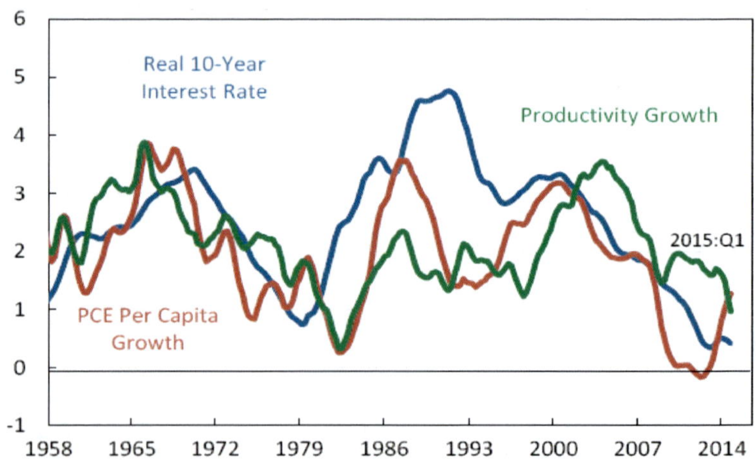

Source: Federal Reserve Board; Bureau of Labor Statistics; Bureau of Economic Analysis.

Figure 6. 10-Year Real Interest Rate, Real Consumption, & Productivity. 20-Quarter Moving Average, Year-over-year Percent Change.

Nonetheless, future long-run productivity growth remains a key driver of understanding the long- term real interest rate, since it is the rate of productivity growth that ultimately pins down the growth rate of all macroeconomic variables including consumption. Views on long-run productivity growth range from extreme optimism about the future to extreme pessimism. Some economists, among them Mokyr (2014), Brynjolfsson and McAfee (2014), and Bloom et al. (2014) point to recent advances in information technology, management techniques, and scientific knowledge as laying the foundation for continued economic growth. They see no reason to think that innovations going forward will be less frequent or contribute less to overall productivity than before. Others, such as Gordon (2010, 2014), are more pessimistic, pointing to the declining quality of public education, pressures of globalization, environmental issues, and government debt as drags on future innovation and growth. And as is discussed further below, others point to secular stagnation—a feedback loop between falling demand and falling investment leading to low interest rates—as a trap that will impede growth in the near- to medium-term. Superficially, there seems to be ample evidence of scientific and technological advance in many dimensions, though there is generally a lag between invention and the development of the production and market infrastructure needed to facilitate an impact of invention on productivity (David and Wright 2006).

One could use time-series methods to estimate the stochastic process driving productivity and forecast out of sample based on the estimated model. There are no easy answers from this approach either. Paralleling the literature on consumption growth, one view is that productivity growth is non-stationary, in which case recent observations on productivity should receive greater weight in the forecast (indeed, on this view, recent productivity could be the best forecast of future productivity). Another view is that productivity growth is mean-reverting, in which case the long-run trend is informative about the future. Yet others argue that productivity growth may follow a switching process, with stochastic shifts between "regimes" of high and low productivity (Kahn and Rich 2011). Again, statistical tests are not dispositive, both because there is insufficient time-series data to identify with any confidence the underlying stochastic process driving productivity and because of challenges in accurately measuring productivity itself.

In the meantime, forecasters must rely on insights from economic models and use their best judgment. Column 1 of Table 1 shows long-run projections of U.S. labor productivity growth, denoted by g, from a variety of studies, including Administration estimates. Productivity estimates range from lows of

1.3 percent per year on the most pessimistic end, to 2.2 percent on the more optimistic end.[14] The most recent long-run Administration forecast is productivity growth of 2.1 percent per year. This forecast is conditional on enactment of Administration policies that include substantial investments in infrastructure, business tax reform, expanded international trade, and increased educational investment.

Most forecasters focus on the nominal interest rate, which can be directly compared with market data. Here, the focus is on the real interest rate and its link with productivity growth. To compare other forecasts with the Ramsey model, we assume (and subtract) an inflation rate of 2.0 percent from nominal interest rate forecasts to obtain a projected long-run real rate (see Column 2 of Table 1). Columns 3 through 5 show different projections for the real interest rate implied by the Ramsey model based on the productivity measures in column 1, and different assumptions about the preference parameters ρ and σ.

The projections for the real interest rate range from 1.5 percent to 3.5 percent. Higher values of ρ and σ generate higher real interest rates. Estimates of labor productivity have a large impact on the forecast of the long-term interest rate.

Table 1. Real Interest Rate Forecasts

			Model-based Forecasts		
			ρ = 0.4	ρ = 0.2	ρ = 0.2
	g	10 year	σ = 1	σ = 1	σ = 1.5
	1	2	3	4	5
Administration	2.1	2.4	2.5	2.3	3.4
Macroeconomic Advisers	1.4	2.3	1.8	1.6	2.3
SSA	2.1	2.9	2.5	2.3	3.4
Fernald	1.6		2.0	1.8	2.6
CBO	1.9	2.6	2.3	2.1	3.1
Gordon	1.3		1.7	1.5	2.2
Byrne, et al.	1.8		2.2	2.0	2.9
Historical	2.2		2.6	2.4	3.5
Average	1.8	2.6	2.2	2.0	2.9
Median	1.9	2.5	2.3	2.1	3.0

Source: Bureau of Labor Statistics; Byrne, et al. (2013); Congressional Budget Office (2015b); Fernald (2014); Gordon (2014); Ma croeconomic Advisers (2015); Social Security Administration (2014).

Note: Historicaldenotes annualized average from 1953:Q2 to 2007:Q4.

Key Takeaways

- The Ramsey growth model implies a link between labor productivity growth, per capita consumption growth and the real (inflation-adjusted) interest rate.
- Historically, periods of low real long-term interest rates have tended to coincide with low labor productivity growth.
- Projections of labor productivity growth, while imprecise, suggest 10-year real interest rates in the range of 1.5 to 3.5 per cent.

III.b. Information from Financial Markets

The price of assets traded in financial markets can provide information about long-run interest rates, but realistic asset-pricing models need to incorporate uncertainty about the future. Appendix B extends the basic growth model to allow for uncertainty in future productivity growth and inflation. The intertemporal marginal rate of substitution (often labeled as the real stochastic discount factor or SDF, $\left(M_{t+1} \equiv \beta u'(c_{t+1})/u'(c_t)\right)$ is central to determining the rate of return on an asset. The key insight from asset pricing theory is that investors care about, and therefore must be compensated for, the risk as well as the timing of asset payoffs. As in the Ramsey model, assets that pay off sooner rather than later are more valuable to the investor and will command a higher price. The value of an asset also depends, however, on whether the payoffs come at a good time or not: an asset that is expected to pay dividends when consumption is relatively low (and therefore the marginal utility of consumption is high) will be more valuable for its insurance benefits than an asset that pays dividends when consumption is already high.

Maintaining previous assumptions about utility and further assuming that the distribution of future SDFs follow a lognormal statistical distribution, the long-term nominal interest rate on date *t* on a discount bond that matures in *k* periods can be approximated as:[15]

$$\begin{aligned} &\tfrac{1}{k}\textstyle\sum_{j=1}^{k} E_t\{r_{t+j}^{1}\} + \\ &\frac{1}{k}\sum_{j=1}^{k} E_t\{\pi_{t+j}\} + \\ &\frac{1}{k}\sum_{j=1}^{k-1} Cov_t\left\{\sigma\left[ln\left(c_{t+j}\right) - ln\left(c_{t+j}\right)\right] + \pi_{t+j}, ln\left(q_{t+j}^{k-j}\right)\right\} \end{aligned} \tag{3}$$

In words, the nominal long-term interest rate depends positively on:

1) Expected future short-term real interest rates, the sequence of r^1_{t+j} (first line of (3)).
2) Expected future inflation rates, the sequence of π_{t+j} (second line of (3)).
3) The term premium (third line of (3)). This reflects two forces:

- The extent to which bond prices tend to vary positively with consumption growth (the covariance between the price of a nominal bond with remaining maturity *k* - *j*, *qk-j*, and contemporaneous consumption growth)
- The extent to which bond prices tend to vary positively with inflation (the covariance between π and *qk-j*, because a bond that has a high value when the value of money is low is less valuable as a hedge).

The first two components on this list correspond to the intuition that investors will compare the interest rate offered by a *k*-period long-term bond with the earnings available from investing instead in a sequence of *k* short-term bonds.[16] Together, the two parts of the term premium reflect the risk associated with holding a long-term bond. Intuitively, a *k*-period bond becomes a (*k* – 1)-period bond after one period, a (*k* – 2)-period bond after two periods, and so on. At any point before maturity, the investor may wish to sell the bond, so in deciding the rate of return she is willing to accept, she will also consider how the future prices of her instrument, as its time to maturity shrinks over the relevant future horizon, covary with consumption and inflation risks.

In addition to these components, the long-term yield may contain at least two other premiums: a credit risk premium and a liquidity premium. The credit premium reflects the risk associated with the solvency of the borrower. Since we are interested in the yield on the long-term U.S Treasury note, the credit risk premium is not relevant.[17] The liquidity premium reflects the risk an investor would face if he or she were unable to sell the bond at fair value due to low market liquidity. Yields on most U.S. Treasuries themselves are unlikely to contain a significant liquidity premium, but such a premium could arise in specific instruments such as inflation indexed bonds, where trading may be thin.

We now turn to financial markets for information about the various components of the long- term interest rate.[18]

Forward Interest Rates

One might hope to glean market expectations of the future long-term interest rate from transactions in bonds of different maturity. An interest rate on a 10-year Treasury note purchased in 2025 and maturing in 2035, for example, can be locked in today by purchasing a 20-year Treasury bond that matures in 2035 and selling the coupon stream from a 10-year Treasury note that matures in 2025. The net cost of that transaction yields a measure of the 10-year interest rate expected to prevail in ten years, which is called the forward interest rate. The rate of return resulting from this transaction is not a pure expected future long-term interest rate, however, as it will carry a risk premium related to the term premiums embedded in the yields of the underlying assets. Nonetheless, the implicit prediction does contain important information about expectations of future rates.

Each line in Figure 7 shows forward rates on a 10-year Treasury note at different horizons. Different lines show the rates that prevailed at different dates. Taking the top (blue) line, for example, the rate at "zero-years" forward is the spot rate on a 10-year Treasury note as of April 2010, a little under 4.0 percent. The rate at "two-years" forward applies to a 10-year Treasury note in April 2012. The July 2015 curve is lower than the April 2010 and December 2013 curves, reflecting the general fall in interest rates between 2010 and 2015 and, probably, the market's view that interest rates are likely to stay lower for some time. The forward market's current implicit prediction for the 10-year nominal rate in 2025 (ten years forward) is 3.1 percent, considerably lower than most forecasters' predictions of the 10-year rate and lower than the 3.6 to 4.7 percent forecasts (real rate plus 2 percent expected inflation) based on the growth model in Table 1.

There are good reasons to be cautious in taking the forward rate as an accurate predictor of the future rate. As noted above, the synthetic forward rate embodies risk premiums; moreover, it relies on prices of assets that may be in very limited supply (for example, the 20-year Treasury). The fact that the market for such securities is thin may lead to pricing anomalies that would affect the forward rate. Empirical analysis of the rate on long-term forwards finds that they are highly volatile and respond to transitory shocks that, from a theoretical perspective, should not affect the long-run interest rate.[19] Thornton and Valente (2012) report that the information contained in forward rates does not provide investors with economic value in terms of higher excess returns relative to an investment strategy based on current information.[20] Thus, the current forward prediction for the 10-year Treasury in 2025 of 3.1 percent is unlikely to be an accurate forecast of the long-term nominal interest rate.

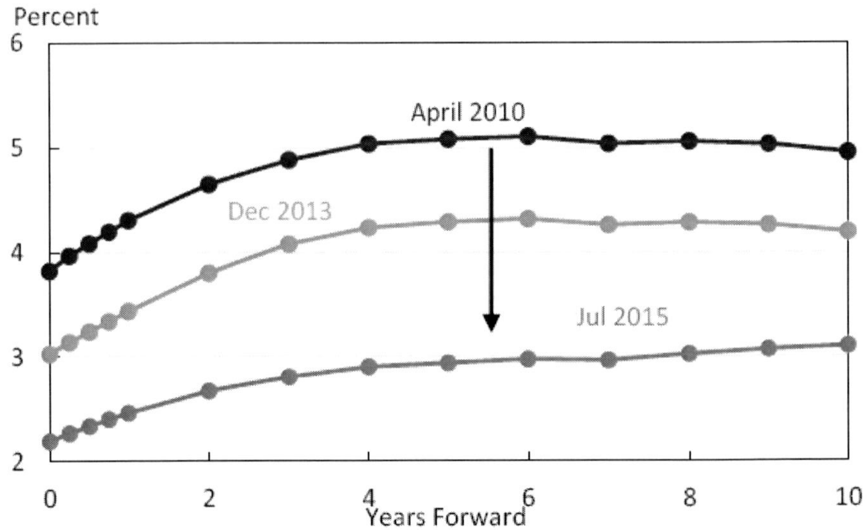

Note: Each dot shows the expected yield on a 10-year treasury note at *x* years forward derived from the yields on 10-20-year Treasury notes.
Source: Bloomberg Professional Service

Figure 7. Market-Implied Evolution of 10-Year Rate Over Time.

TIPS (Treasury Inflation-Protected Securities)

The market for TIPS was established in 1997 and now accounts for roughly 8.5 percent of the volume of outstanding Treasuries. TIPS are indexed to the CPI and so provide an investor a real return insured against inflation in that price index.21 Figure 8 shows the annual yield on the 10- year TIPS up through July 2015, and from July 2015 through July 2025, the annual yield based on forwards on TIPS. As of July 2015, the implied annual real yield on the 10-year TIPS was 0.3 percent. Forward transactions like those described for nominal bonds imply a 10-year TIPS rate of 1.0 percent in ten years. The return on 10-year TIPS is a measure of expected real interest rates (reflected in the first component of equation (3)) plus a term premium. In some conditions, the yield on TIPS may also include a liquidity premium. Even with these additional premiums, the real yield on TIPS is broadly consistent with the real yield on nominal Treasury bonds implied by forward transactions, given the Federal Reserve's inflation target; and, like that yield, real yields on TIPS are considerably lower than the real return implied by the growth model explored earlier. Alternatively and equivalently, the ten-year ahead nominal 10-year rate implied by forward transactions in TIPS is about 3.25 percent (the sum of the 1.00 percent forward yield on TIPS plus 2.25 percent expected CPI inflation), compared with the implicit prediction of 3.10 percent derived from nominal Treasuries.

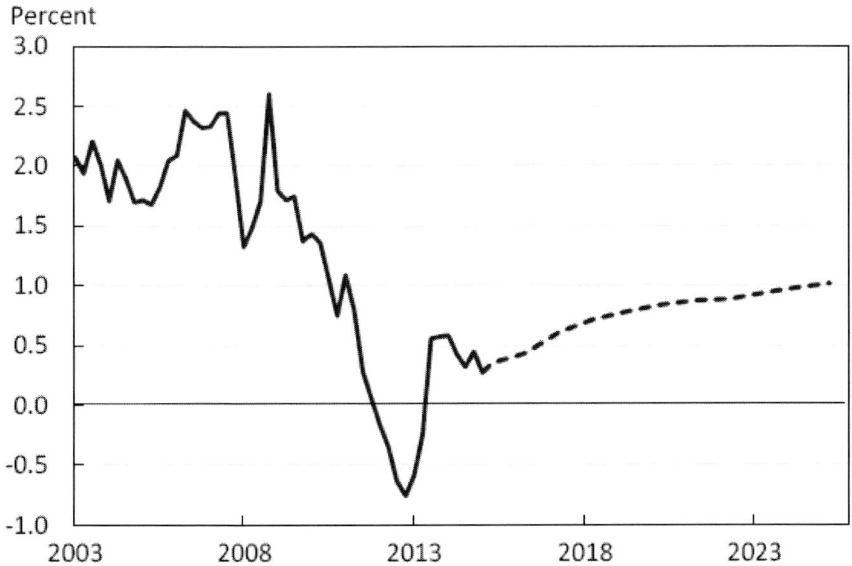

Note: Dotted line indicates TIPS forward yields as of July 8, 2015.
Source: Federal Reserve Board; Bloomberg Service.

Figure 8. 10-Year Treasury Inflation Protected Security Yield.

As with forwards on nominal Treasuries, a number of caveats should be kept in mind when interpreting forward rates on TIPS. In addition to a term premium, the yield on TIPS may also include a liquidity premium due to thin trading volume. Empirical analysis suggests that both of these premiums vary over time. D'Amico et al. (2014) find that as the market for TIPS expanded in the early 2000s, the liquidity premium declined followed by a spike during the financial crisis.

FOMC Participant Assessments of Short-Term Interest Rates

The Federal Open Market Committee (FOMC) publishes the distribution of its members' assessment for the future federal funds rate. The federal funds rate, technically the rate at which depository institutions lend to each other on an overnight basis, reflects the short-term real rate plus expected inflation. The FOMC's median assessment for the Fed funds rate over the longer run is currently 3.75 percent. The relationship between the federal funds rate and the U.S. Treasury rate is historically stable—the federal funds rate tends to exceed the three-month Treasury rate by approximately 12 to 15 basis points.[22] Thus, the FOMC longer-run assessments suggest a short-term nominal Treasury rate in 2025 of about 3.6 percent. The implied level of the 10-year rate in 2025 would be substantially higher after the addition of a projected 1.0 percent term premium, and therefore substantially above the 3.1 percent implicit prediction from forward Treasury transactions, as we discuss further below.

Term Premium

The term premium reflects the extra return that lenders demand holding a longer-term bond instead of investing in a series of short-term securities. In theory, the sign and size of the term premium depend on the covariance between bond prices and other factors that affect the investor's wealth (see Cox et al. 1985). If bonds are a good hedge for other risks the investor might face, such as inflation, changes in wages, or the returns on other assets in the investor's portfolio, the term premium can be low or even negative.

The term premium is not directly observable and numerous strategies have been developed to estimate it by imposing restrictions on the stochastic properties of the data or by utilizing other data, such as survey information, to provide identification. Adrian et al. (2013) use econometric techniques to decompose the nominal rate on 10-year Treasury notes into the expected future path of short-term Treasury yields and the term premium.[23] Figure 9 shows the yield on 10-year Treasuries and the term premium based on their methodology. Daily changes in the term premium and the aggregate yield are highly positively correlated (correlation coefficient of 0.72) over the full sample. There are periods, however, when the two series diverge (such as 2007-09). The term premium has tended to fall along with the decline in the long-term interest rate, and Adrian et al. estimate that it is currently negative.[24] D'Amico et al. (2014) and Campbell et al. (2013) also find evidence of a negative term premium.

The low term premium suggests that long-term bonds add little risk, and indeed may add diversification, to the set of risks currently faced by investors. The difficult question for an interest-rate forecast is what will happen to term premiums ten to twenty years into the future. Some models of the term premium (see for example, Kim and Wright (2005)) include a mean- reverting component. Simply projecting that model forward generates a long-run term premium of approximately 0.80 percentage point, driven by increases in both the real term premium and the inflation risk premium from their current low levels. Because the Kim-Wright model is a non- structural statistical model, however, this projection does not take into account changes in macroeconomic conditions and their potentially time-varying covariance with financial variables.

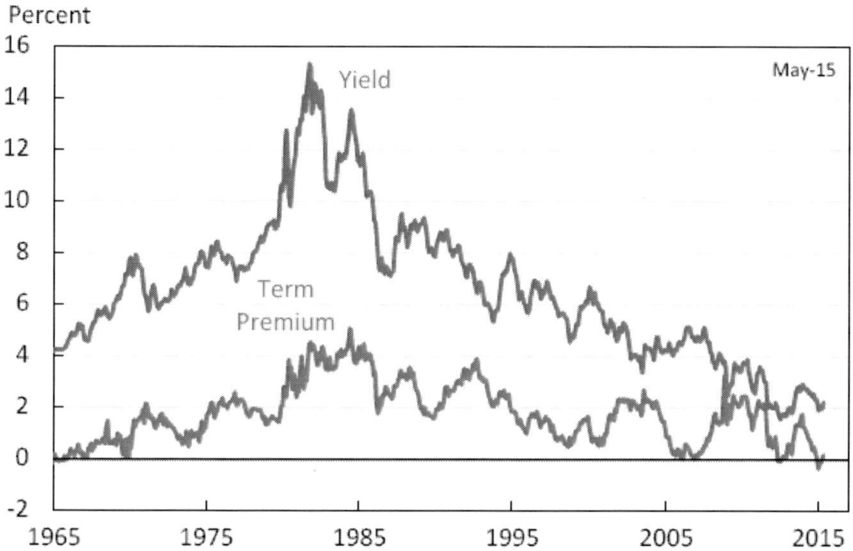

Source: Federal Reserve Board; Federal Reserve Bank of New York, http://www.newyorkfed.org/research/data_indicators/term_premia.html.

Figure 9. 10-Year Yield and Term Premium.

To gain some insight into the underlying economic forces that seem to be driving the term premium, and therefore help predict it going forward, Adrian et al. (2013) use historical data to seek correlated economic factors. They find that term premiums appear to be high when unemployment is high, when there is increased dispersion in professional forecasts about future bond yields, and when options-implied volatility suggests high uncertainty about Treasury yields. Interestingly, they find little evidence that term premiums rise when monetary policy tightens. Taken together, this evidence suggests that term premiums could remain low if expectations about inflation remain well-anchored as the economy continues to expand.

Campbell et al. (2009) note that much of the variation in the inflation premium remains unexplained by the factors in their model. They suggest that other variables not in their current specification, such as the supply of Treasury bonds, may be important for bond term premiums (see also Krishnamurthy and Vissing-Jorgenson 2011, 2012 and Li and Wei 2013). This latter point could be important if the demand for safe assets were to change going forward. Ang et al. (2008) find that the variation in inflation compensation (expected inflation and its covariance risk with consumption growth) explains about 80 percent of the variation in nominal rates at both short and long maturities. This underscores the point that small changes in the perception of inflation risk could have a sizable impact on long-term interest rates.

Of all of the components of nominal long-term interest rates, the value for the term premium is the most difficult to pin down. In the table below, the mean of the Adrian et al. (2013) term premium over the January 1, 2005 to December 31, 2014 period of 1.0 percentage point is used.

Summarizing the Information from Financial Markets

To illustrate our analyses, we illustrate different approaches to forecasting the long-term nominal interest rate, as is typically done twice a year in the CEA/OMB/Treasury Budget forecast and mid- session review. Table 2 summarizes the market information on the various components of the expected long-term nominal interest rate. Forward nominal Treasury interest rates suggest a rate of 3.10 percent. The forecast based on TIPS plus expected CPI inflation would suggest a rate of 3.25 percent that could likewise include a bias due to term and liquidity premiums. The FOMC federal funds rate assessment, adjusted to provide an implicit short-term Treasury rate forecast and adding a 1.00 percentage point term premium, implies a long-term forecast of 4.60 percent.

Table 2. Components of Nominal Interest Rate based on Financial Data

	(1) Short-Term Real (1-Year)	(2) Expected Inflation	(3) + (4) Term Premium	FORECAST 10-Year
Forward Treasuries	3.10			3.10
TIPS	1.00	2.25		3.25
FOMC-Based	3.60		1.00	4.60
Blue Chip				4.40

Although reached through different reasoning, the rate on the 10-year Treasury note suggested by the FOMC's funds rate forecast is in the same neighborhood as that based on the steady-state prediction of a Ramsey model. This is not surprising—if the Ramsey model is a valid description of the economy, long-run interest rates and market expectations about the future will ultimately conform to the equilibrium conditions in the Ramsey model. There is a gap, however, between the rate implied by the Ramsey model presented here—which includes neither inflation risk nor uncertainty and therefore does not include a term premium—and the rate implied by financial markets, which in principle incorporate all risks but could be strongly affected by current economic conditions. Bringing the rate implied by the macro model into conformance with the rate implied by financial markets (e.g., the 4.4 percent nominal rate implied by Table 1 plus a term premium with the 4.6 percent FOMC-based forecast in Table 2 that includes the term premium) requires either a small or even negative term premium, a lower expected productivity growth rate that would reduce the Ramsey-implied rate, or a higher elasticity of intertemporal substitution (lower σ) than seems realistic to most economists.

Key Takeaways

- Asset-pricing models that incorporate risk suggest that the long-run nominal interest rate is the sum of expected future short-term real rates, expected future inflation rates, and a term premium.
- The 10-year rate in ten years that forward transactions in nominal Treasuries imply is currently 3.1 percent.
- Forward transactions in the market for TIPS suggest a long-term real rate just above 1.00 percent in ten years. Adding the CPI inflation rate implied by the Federal Reserve's PCE inflation target would imply a forward nominal interest rate of 3.25 percent.
- The term premium in nominal Treasuries is currently estimated to be near zero, with a 2005-2014 mean of 1 percent.
- These components together suggest a 10-year nominal interest rate in the range of 3.1 (forward Treasuries) to 4.6 percent (based on FOMC forecasts of the long-run federal funds rate).

III.c. Real Interest Rates in a Globalized World Economy

In a closed economy, all of the aggregate economy's saving necessarily flows into domestic investment. In an open economy, saving also can flow into assets located abroad (when the economy has a current account surplus); or foreign borrowing may allow the economy to invest more than it is currently saving (when the economy has a current account deficit).

At a basic level, the real interest rate in a closed economy is determined by the equality of national saving and domestic investment.[25] In a world with financially integrated national capital markets, the general level of world interest rates is determined by the equality of the *global* supply of saving and *global* investment demand—with individual countries' current account balances determined by whether domestic saving exceeds or falls short of national investment in the global capital-market equilibrium.

An extensive literature in international finance tests for the degree of integration of national financial markets.[26] The general consensus of this literature is that advanced economies have tightly integrated capital markets, emerging market economies are becoming increasingly integrated into the global financial system, while China (through deliberate policy choices that restrict capital movements) and low-income economies remain partially segmented from the global capital market. Even for the advanced economies, real interest rates need not be precisely equal across borders, even at long horizons, thanks to several factors including exchange-rate fluctuations. Increasingly, however, arbitrage forces tend to make long-term real and even nominal interest rates move in tandem. Figure 10, inspired by Blanchard et al. (2014), shows the narrowing spread in long-term nominal interest rates across OECD countries that has occurred since the 1980s as well as the accompanying decline in those rates.[27] Figure 11 shows a specific recent short-term example, the close co-movement in U.S. and German 10-year government bond rates over most sub-periods after September 2014 despite different macroeconomic conditions and monetary policies in the United States and the euro area. Long-term nominal interest rates in Europe and Japan have recently been mostly below those in the United States, and current rates on 10-year bonds even fall short of inflation in Japan, France, Canada, Sweden, and Denmark.[28]

One explanation for the global decline in interest rates is that the same forces driving down the U.S. rate are operating abroad. According to the IMF (International Monetary Fund 2014), a common global factor accounted for 55 percent of the variation in world interest rates over 1980-1995 and this share increased to almost 75 percent during 1996-2012.[29] Note that the band in Figure 10 widens after the onset of the global financial crisis in 2007, reflecting diverging economic conditions across countries, the consequent differences in central bank monetary policies, and the unraveling of sovereign yield convergence in the euro area. Over the longer run, however, the general trend of narrowing differences across countries, reflected in the width of the gray band in Figure 10, suggests that while common factors may be at work, increased financial integration across markets has indeed pulled interest rates together.

Given the global equilibrium real interest rate, an extension of the Ramsey model would tie the growth rate of every country's per capita consumption to that interest rate via equation (2), while divergences between countries' overall spending and output levels would be resolved through external lending or borrowing. In the world capital-market equilibrium, the global real interest rate ultimately depends on the productivity growth rates of all the world's economies, with each country's contribution weighted by its importance in world GDP.

This mechanism leads to some convergence of national real rates of interest, but what about nominal rates? Given real convergence, the tendency of countries in recent decades to adopt inflation-targeting regimes with somewhat similar target inflation rates or ranges has also promoted convergence of long-term nominal rates. Japan's experience, illustrated in Figure 4 above, shows how divergent inflation expectations (in Japan's case, decades of expectations of very low or negative inflation) can lead to divergence in long-term nominal interest rates.

Through the mechanism of integrated international markets, foreign factors also influence a country's *natural* real rate of interest, the rate consistent with full employment in the absence of short-term cyclical fluctuations. Central banks typically adjust their policy rates in an attempt to track the natural rate. Because the latter is subject to strong global influences, the fact that short- term nominal policy rates follow long-term rates over the long-run, even though the latter are heavily influenced by foreign developments, does not imply that the central bank lacks policy tools with which to steer the economy. Rather, effective domestic monetary policy requires the central bank to respond to global factors that simultaneously affect long-term interest rates.

In a world with uncertainty, global long-term real and nominal interest rates will naturally include risk premiums. An individual country's rates depend in part on idiosyncratic, purely national, factors. Common international patterns in the linkages between national consumption levels and world interest rates can, however, induce substantial correlation among countries' long-term bond risk premiums.

The generally higher output and consumption growth rates in the emerging and developing world, which have become an ever-bigger fraction of the world economy over time, might be considered by some observers as evidence for higher interest rates in the United States and other rich countries than are suggested by their own growth rates alone. The transmission of rates from the extensive and deep financial markets of the industrial countries to those of poorer countries is still much more powerful, however, than the reverse transmission. Moreover, systematic differences in long-term growth rates can be accommodated by systematic trends in real exchange rates that drive a wedge between different countries' real interest rates, without necessarily muting much of the correlation between changes in these interest rates. (For example, China's currency has appreciated against the dollar in real terms over time.) Appendix D discusses this linkage. Finally, as discussed in the next section, growth projections for emerging markets have been revised downward recently, contributing to the falling trend in global interest rates.

Key Takeaways

- In a world with financially integrated national capital markets, the general level of world interest rates is determined by the equality of the global supply of saving and global investment demand.
- Capital markets of advanced economies are now tightly integrated while emerging market economies are becoming increasingly integrated into the global financial system. Low- income economies remain partially segmented from the global capital market.
- As a consequence of increasing international market integration, long-term real and nominal interest rates are increasingly moving in tandem and have declined along with U.S. rates. Nominal interest rates also tend to be correlated across countries though differences in inflation expectations can produce differences in nominal rates.
- In a world with uncertainty, global long-term real and nominal interest rates will include risk premiums that can reflect country-specific risk factors. Strong economic linkages, however, reinforce substantial correlation in countries' long-term bond risk premiums.

IV. Why Have Interest Rates Fallen So Much?

Interest rates in the United States are very low today, with real 10-year interest rates essentially at zero. Most observers believe that this is, at least in part, a transitory phenomenon and that interest rates will rise as the economy fully recovers and monetary policy normalizes. Further, some believe that this transitory reduction has been especially deep and prolonged because of unique factors associated with the aftermath of a severe financial crisis.

Nevertheless, expected future long-term interest rates a decade from now have also fallen substantially from what was expected by forecasters, or indicated by market forward rates, a decade or two ago. That decline suggests there may also be structural changes in the economy that will lead to lower equilibrium long-term interest rates even when the economy is fully recovered. Determining how long low long-term interest rates will persist and whether they will settle at a lower level than previously expected requires an evaluation of the reasons they are low today. While there is no definitive answer to this question, many factors suggest that long- run equilibrium long-term interest rates have fallen.

Factors that Are Likely Transitory

Fiscal, Monetary, and Foreign-Exchange Policies

The recent recession saw the expansion of public balance sheets, in some cases because private debt was absorbed by national governments. If consumers are Ricardian—that is, they do not consider their government debt holdings to be net wealth because they fully anticipate paying the future taxes the government will levy to service its debts—the effects of higher deficits (dissaving) by the government are undone by increased saving on the part of private agents, who anticipate higher future taxes due to the higher deficit.[30] In this scenario, reduced government budget deficits do not raise aggregate saving and therefore have no impact on the interest rate. The stark assumptions of Ricardian equivalence do not hold if, more realistically, people are finitely lived (without an operative bequest motive) or do not fully anticipate future tax liabilities. Thus, one might have expected the higher public debt levels in the post-crisis period to push long- term interest rates *higher* and thereby crowd out capital (unless, once again, Ricardian equivalence holds).

One reason why such pressure on long-term interest rates has not been observed may be that in the case of the largest economies (the United States and United Kingdom, and then in Japan and Europe), large-scale programs of quantitative easing have moved public (and often private) long- term debts from private to central-bank balance sheets, reducing long-term interest rates. Central banks in emerging markets have continued to purchase foreign exchange reserves, mostly U.S. government-issued or government-backed securities. Rogoff (2015) argues that another factor depressing interest rates in some countries is “financial repression” under which governments artificially depress government-bond interest rates so as to liquidate high public debts more rapidly. In addition, after the increase in public debt that accompanied the financial crisis and recession, many advanced-country governments pursued policies aimed at reducing structural fiscal deficits, likely placing further downward pressure on interest rates.

Inflation Risk and the Term Premium

At present the term premium is at historic lows, and estimates show it has even touched negative values (see Figure 9 above). The term premium captures the extent to which long-term bond prices provide a hedge against consumption risks (see Appendix B). A negative term premium could reflect a negative covariance between the real economy and bond prices, such that bond prices tend to rise when the news about consumption growth is bad. In this case, nominal long- term bonds provide a "deflation hedge" (Campbell et al. 2013)—an effect that seems most likely when, as has been the case since the financial crisis, nominal interest rates are very low and the ambient price environment is one of deflation pressures. Historically, term premiums have tended to be at higher levels than today's, and to the extent that low premiums result from the current set of cyclical circumstances and policy responses, they should eventually normalize at historical levels.

Private-Sector Deleveraging

The decade leading up to the financial crisis saw a global liquidity boom in which households in many countries took on unprecedented levels of debt while financial institutions sharply increased their leverage. The collapse in asset values and the recession in 2007-09 initiated a period of higher household saving aimed at paying down debts, as well as balance sheet consolidation by financial institutions facing a more stringent regulatory climate. Reinhart and Rogoff (2009) argue that recessions in the aftermath of financial crises tend to be more severe and more persistent than typical business-cycle recessions, although they eventually come to an end once household and business balance sheets are healthy. Not only does the deleveraging process discourage consumption and thereby push down real interest rates, it tends to be associated with deflationary pressures that depress long-term nominal interest rates, both directly (through the inflation-expectations channel) and indirectly (through monetary policy responses).[31]

Rogoff (2015) has recently re-stated the view that the advanced economies are still experiencing negative growth effects from an abruptly and disruptively terminated long credit cycle. As one piece of evidence, he points to lower loan availability for borrowers with less-than-stellar credit profiles, a factor that has notably been holding back residential borrowing in the United States. Hamilton et al. (2015) argue similarly. The Bank for International

Settlements (BIS) has long espoused a closely related view, restated in its latest annual report (2015), which could explain not only currently low interest rates but their worldwide decline since the 1980s. Throughout the world, financial innovation and liberalization, coupled with imperfect macro- and micro- prudential regulation, led to credit expansion and downward pressure on interest rates, culminating in the global credit surge of the 2000s and the resulting global financial crisis. Post- crisis, central banks have held interest rates low to offset the contractionary effects of ongoing deleveraging. The BIS recommends that countries raise policy interest rates in concert with structural reforms.

Factors that Are Likely Longer-lived

Lower Global Long-run Output and Productivity Growth

The Ramsey model emphasized the link between saving and productivity growth. A fall in expected future output and income growth makes people feel less wealthy and induces them to save more today, with the aggregate response pushing down the real interest rate. It is therefore notable that across all regions of the world, growth expectations have declined in recent years.

Table 3 shows OECD projections of growth in real per capita GDP and total factor productivity through 2034. In all regions, including the global aggregate, growth is expected to pick up over the next decade relative to the sluggish 2010-14 period. However, growth in the following decade, which is the relevant period for the long-run forecast, is expected to be somewhat lower. In particular, the rapid growth in China and other parts of Asia that characterized the past two decades is anticipated to taper off, and authors such as Pritchett and Summers (2014) argue that the tapering could be very rapid. These forecasts of future growth, taken at face value, are not supportive of a large increase in the real interest rate.

Since the financial crisis, growth forecasts published by the IMF, OECD, and World Bank have been progressively downgraded, as illustrated for the IMF forecasts in Figure 12. Much of the downgrade reflects escalating concerns about future productivity growth, and whether lower productivity growth should be viewed as a temporary or longer-lived phenomenon is the subject of heated debate among historians and economists, as Section III above described.

Table 3. Global GDP and Total Factor Productivity Growth

	Annualized Percent Change in Real GDP per Capita			Annualized Percent Change in Total Factor Productivity		
	2010-2014	2014-2024	2024-2060	2010-2014	2014-2024	2024-2060
World	2.4	2.9	2.3			
OECD	1.1	2.0	1.6	1.0	0.9	0.6
USA	1.5	2.0	1.3	1.0	0.9	0.7
Euro Zone	0.1	1.7	1.6	1.0	0.9	0.6
Emerging Markets*	5.0	4.3	3.0	0.9	0.8	0.5

Source : OECD Economic Outlook 2014 - Long-term baseline projections
*Brazil, China, India, Indonesia, Russia, South Africa

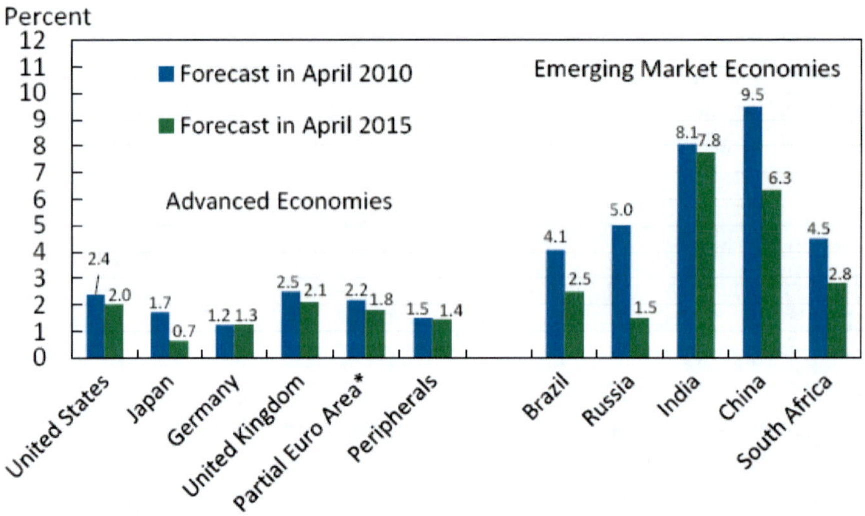

Note: *Partial Euro Area excludes Germany and Peripheral countries. Peripheral countries are
Greece, Ireland, Italy, Portugal, and Spain.
Source: International Monetary Fund, World Economic Outlook April 2010 and April 2015; CEA Calculations.

Figure 12. Five-Year-Ahead Growth Forecasts in Selected.

Shifting Demographics

The interest rate in the Ramsey model is based on the assumption that savers care about the infinite future, in that members value their descendants' consumption as though it were their own future consumption. More realistically, people's preferences about consumption and saving change over the life cycle, with middle-aged individuals tending to save in advance of retirement while younger individuals tend to take on debt to finance the purchase of a home or college tuition. Depending on the age distribution of the economy and the overall rate of population growth, the amount of saving and investment will vary, as will the real interest rate. In the United States, the anticipated increase in the ratio of high-saving middle-aged cohort (ages 40 to 49) relative to the high-spending young cohort (ages 20-29) is forecasted to depress U.S. interest rates in the coming decade (see Favero et al. 2013, which extends the model in Geanakoplos et al. 2004).

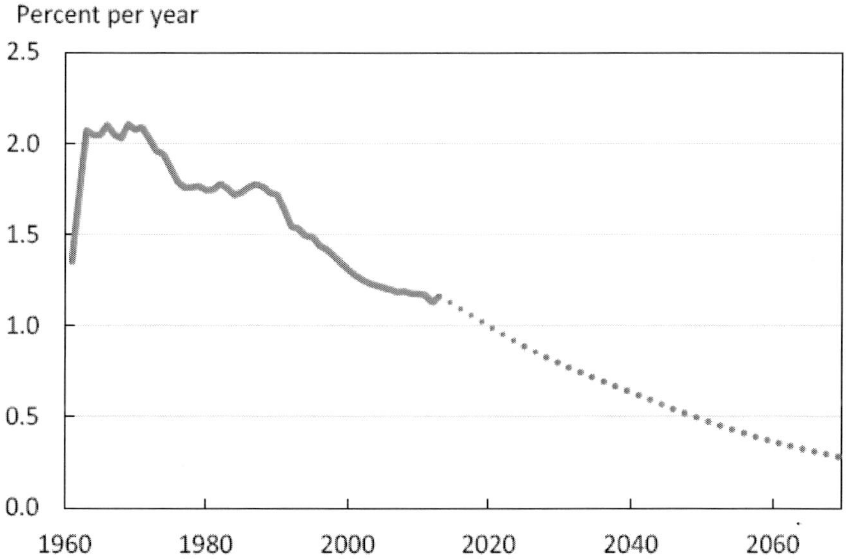

Source: The World Bank; The United Nations.

Figure 13. World Population Growth Rate.

Of course, global demographic trends, by influencing long-term interest rates abroad, will also affect U.S. rates. Projections suggest that the world population growth rate is expected to decline by 0.25 percentage points between 2010 and 2024, and to continue thereafter (see Figure 13). Declining population growth is likely to have a negative effect on productivity growth through several channels. More slowly growing populations reduce the incentives to incur the fixed costs of R&D and innovation; they imply reduced effects of scale on the generation of new knowledge; and they imply slower growth in the adoption of productivity-enhancing innovations. Moreover, less investment is needed to equip a more slowly growing labor force with new capital, an additional channel that can lower long-run interest rates in models with demographic structures more complex than in the Ramsey model. Thus, declining population growth is another force that may depress long-term interest rates.

The Global "Saving Glut"

One explanation for current low global real interest rates is that the world saving curve has shifted outward, driving down the world interest rate. Such a shift puts downward pressure on global interest rates, inducing global investment to rise until, in equilibrium, it is once again equal to global saving. Motivating the upward shift in saving could be the possible expectations of lower future productivity growth just described, which would tend to raise saving and lower real interest rates, as well as factors emphasized by Bernanke (2005) in his original exposition of the "global saving glut" hypothesis, which emphasized precautionary reserve accumulation by emerging market governments. Of course, post-crisis deleveraging has also played a role.

Figure 14 below shows saving and investment rates for advanced economies, emerging markets, and the world as a whole based on the IMF's forecast through 2019. Global saving and investment rose sharply starting in the early 2000s, fell sharply in the financial crisis (when saving and investment demand both collapsed) but then resumed an upward climb. Looking forward, the IMF projects a continued upward trend in saving and investment for some years. If data measurement were perfect, global saving would equal global investment exactly. Accordingly, it is not the gap (which reflects measurement error) but the levels of both series that are of interest. The question is whether the upward trend is primarily due to rising investment demand, which would increase the world interest rate, or to increasing world saving, which would depress the rate. Because world saving and investment must be equal, an observed increase in these series could in principle reflect some combination of a rise in desired saving and a rise in desired investment. The downward trend of falling real interest rates throughout the world is evidence that the forces leading to higher saving may have been dominant in the past, and that could remain the case going forward.

The gap between saving and investment in emerging markets was especially large in the 2000s, contributing to emerging-market current account surpluses and the "global saving glut" that Bernanke (2005) argued helped to fuel global current-account imbalances and asset bubbles in financial markets.

As already noted, among the factors that explain the expanded pool of saving in that epoch are increased precautionary saving by emerging economies in the wake of the late-1990s Asian crisis and one of its symptoms, the strong demand for reserves on the part of emerging-market central banks. Since the recent financial crisis, the emerging-market gap has declined and the IMF projects it will be near zero by the end of 2019. However, global saving overall is on the rise, driven largely by higher saving in advanced economies. If higher saving is driven by lower expected future productivity growth, and if that lower growth is a long-term phenomenon, then the upward trend of saving the IMF projects in Figure 14 could be associated with a considerable period of continuing downward pressure on global interest rates.

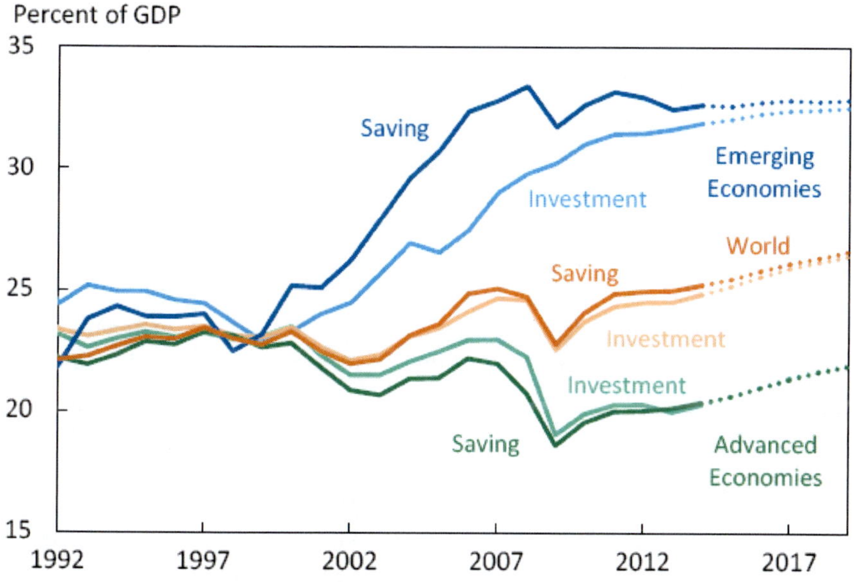

Note: Dotted lines indicate forecasts.
Source: International Monetary Fund.

Figure 14. Global Saving and Investment, 1992–2019.

Safe Asset Shortage

Caballero (2006) argued even before the global financial crisis that the supply of relatively safe assets was failing to keep up with global demand for those assets—as savings vehicles, for collateral, and for other purposes. Bernanke (2005) stressed that safe asset demand by central banks (i.e., for foreign exchange reserves) had contributed to global current-account imbalances.

In contrast, Caballero argued that the problem was not an ex ante excess of global saving over investment, but an ex ante portfolio mismatch between the assets savers desired and those available in the market.

Caballero (2010) argued further that U.S. financial market innovation responded to the global safe asset shortage by manufacturing synthetic safe assets in the form of AAA tranches of securitized loan portfolios—thereby helping set the stage for the global financial crisis. The realization that such securities may not, in fact, be safe has reinforced the safe asset shortage.

The euro zone crisis has also raised the riskiness of some government bonds previously considered safe. The excess demand for safe assets thus seems unlikely to abate any time soon.

Secular Stagnation?

An influential recent account of current low interest rates is the "secular stagnation" hypothesis espoused by Summers (2014). According to this theory, weak aggregate demand and a lack of productive investment opportunities has shifted the economy into a state of persistent stagnation at very low, if not negative, real interest rates.

Under this theory, with nominal interest rates at the lower bound of zero and inflation expectations governed by a price-stability target, monetary policy may lack the capacity to maintain full employment or even to counter deflation expectations, which push the real interest rate away from its natural or full-employment level.

The equilibrium persists because low investment and unemployment of labor themselves reduce the economy's productive capacity through a deterioration of the quality of human and physical capital. Long-term nominal interest rates are very low although the real rate need not be low if sufficiently high deflation expectations become entrenched. If low interest rates generate asset-price bubbles, investment will increase and the economy can attain full employment, but only at the risk of financial instability threats.

It seems doubtful that a secular stagnation model applies currently to the United States, though the case arguably is stronger in other parts of the world. Two pieces of evidence weigh against the secular stagnation argument for the United States.

First, Hamilton et al. (2015) present empirical evidence that U.S. aggregate demand has not been sustained primarily by bubbles in recent decades.

Second, as pointed out by Bernanke (2015), the forces of globalization weaken the potential for secular stagnation. In an integrated global economy, productive investment opportunities anywhere in the world will push global interest rates upward and tend to counter stagnation at home as capital flows outward, depreciating the currency and raising exports. That depreciation redistributes among countries the higher global demand caused by one economy's enhanced investment opportunities. Bernanke (2015) argues, in addition, that the saving glut he detected in the 2000s may be moderating, which would tend to push global interest rates upward. If the IMF forecasts of future global saving trends cited earlier are right, the increases will be driven increasingly by investment demand.

One element pushing against the view that nominal interest rates will be depressed in the long term is the stock of potential high-return infrastructure investment opportunities throughout the world, especially in the emerging countries with growing middle classes (Kharas 2010). It was on this basis that McKinsey Global Institute (2010) forecast an eventual reversal of low global interest rates.

Another factor suggesting higher real and nominal interest rates in the future is the likelihood, discussed above, that the current slowdown in productivity growth represents a pause rather than a permanent state of affairs due to the low likelihood of new inventions as significant as those of the past. However, some emerging markets face governance and other problems that impede efficient infrastructure investment, whereas the time horizon over which current scientific and technical advances will feed into higher productivity growth is uncertain. Thus, it is unclear how much counterweight the preceding factors can provide against other forces pointing to persistently lower long-term interest rates.

Tail Risks and Fundamental Uncertainty

The simple asset pricing formula in (3) focused on average risks and their covariances, but suppressed higher-order convexity terms that could capture "tail risks"—that is, extreme events that occur with very low probability but could have devastating consequences. The possibility of low-risk catastrophes can significantly depress long-term real interest rates, especially when market participants must use estimation procedures to assess the possible magnitudes and probabilities of those risks. (Weitzman 2009 gives a seminal analysis of such "unknown unknowns," applied to the possibility climate catastrophes. Barro 2013 explores an alternative framework.)

The presence of large potential consumption declines with hard-to-estimate likelihoods can greatly increase the subjective variability of future consumption growth, inducing substantial precautionary saving that pushes real interest rates down.

In the United States, sharply reduced volatility in inflation and growth led economists to call the period from roughly the mid-1980s until 2007 the "great moderation" (see Stock and Watson 2003, who ascribed the change to better monetary policy). Since then, however, market participants have become aware of the possibility of financial instability on a scale sufficient to cause a deep and prolonged global economic slowdown. Moreover, markets also face heightened tail risks due to continuing environmental risks, new cyber threats, difficulties in containing virulent infectious disease outbreaks, and intensified geopolitical instability. One result could be lower long-term interest rates, and most probably persistently lower, because many of these risks seem unlikely to recede soon.

The tail-risk hypothesis by itself cannot explain the declining trend of interest rates that began during the great moderation period (Figure 1), but it does imply a lowering of long-term interest rates relative to earlier levels.

Key Takeaways

- Long-term interest rates are lower now than they were thirty years ago, reflecting an outward shift in the global supply curve of saving relative to global investment demand. It remains an open question whether the underlying factors producing current low rates are transitory, or imply long-run equilibrium long-term interest rates lower than before the financial crisis.
- Factors that are likely to dissipate over time—and therefore could lead to higher rates in the future—include current fiscal, monetary, and exchange rate policies; low-inflation risk as reflected in the term premium; and private-sector deleveraging in the aftermath of the global financial crisis.
- Factors that are more likely to persist—suggesting that low interest rates could be a long-run phenomenon—include lower forecasts of global output and productivity growth, demographic shifts, global demand for safe assets outstripping supply, and the impact of tail risks and fundamental uncertainty.

V. CONCLUSION

Many factors play roles in the determination of long-term interest rates, including the rate of productivity growth, beliefs about future risks, consumer preferences, demographic shifts, and the stances of monetary and fiscal policy. As markets have become globally integrated, conditions in foreign markets are increasingly important for U.S. long-term interest rates. Over the past two decades, long-term interest rates have been falling worldwide. An explanation for why they are so low—and whether those low levels will persist—is one of the most difficult questions facing macroeconomists today.

Interest rates are jointly determined by the supply of saving and the demand for investment. While it is difficult to make strong predictions, this report argues that there are a number of reasons to think that the global saving supply curve has shifted outward, a development that would help to keep equilibrium interest rates low.

As with any price in the economy, a low price is beneficial to some and has negative ramifications for others. Low long-term interest rates make it cheaper for governments to finance their debt burdens. By reducing the cost of borrowing, lower long-term interest rates create more fiscal space for government programs, including infrastructure investment, reducing the cost of expansionary fiscal policy. Lower long-term interest rates should also reduce the cost of borrowing by the private sector, encouraging investments that can enhance growth in the future. However, if rates are low because of subdued expectations about future growth, investment is unlikely to be robust.

For savers, lower equilibrium long-term interest rates would affect the return to savings, the cost of borrowing for homeownership, and lifecycle decisions about when to retire and the time pattern of consumption.

Finally, lower long-term interest rates could have important implications for monetary policy, particularly regarding the zero lower bound for short-term interest rates and specific policy tools. Market participants, in turn, may take these factors into effect when making economic forecasts or planning consumption and investment.

Ultimately, interest rates reflect fundamental macroeconomic conditions and there is no "optimal" rate of interest. The goal of policy should not be to target a particular rate, but to support long-run growth, maintain price stability, and strengthen the resilience of financial markets.

References

Adrian, Tobias, Richard K. Crump, and Emanuel Moench. 2013. "Pricing the Term Structure with Linear Regressions." *Federal Reserve Bank of New York Staff Report 340*: 1-66.

Ang, Andrew, Geert Bekaert, and Min Wei. 2008. "The Term Structure of Real Rates and Expected Inflation." *Journal of Finance*, 63(2), 797-849.

Bank for International Settlements. 2015. *85th Annual Report, 2014/15.*

Barro, Robert J. 2013. "Environmental Protection, Rare Disasters, and Discount Rates." *NBER Working Paper*, 19258.

Bernanke, Ben S. 2005. "The Global Saving Glut and the U.S. Current Account Deficit." *The Sandridge Lecture*, Virginia Association of Economists, Richmond, VA, March 10. http://www.federalreserve.gov/boarddocs/speeches/2005/200503102/.

____ 2015. "Why Are Interest Rates So Low, Part 3: The Global Savings Glut." *Ben Bernanke's Blog*, April 1. http://www.brookings.edu/blogs/ben-bernanke/posts/2015/04/01-why-interest-rates-low-global-savings-glut.

Blanchard, Olivier J., Davide Furceri, and Andrea Pescatori. 2014. "A Prolonged Period of Low Real Interest Rates?" In Coen Teulings and Richard Baldwin, eds., *Secular Stagnation: Facts, Causes and Cures*, Centre for Economic Policy Research, London, UK.

Bloom, Nicholas, Erik Brynjolfsson, Lucia Foster, Ron S. Jarmin, Megha Patnaik, Itay Saporta- Eksten, and John Van Reenen. 2014. "IT and Management in America." *CEPR Discussion Paper*, DP9886.

Brynjolfsson, Erik and Andrew McAfee. 2014. *The Second Machine Age: Work, Progress, and Prosperity in a Time of Brilliant Technologies*, Norton, New York.

Byrne, Joseph P., Stephen D. Oliner, and Daniel E. Sichel. 2013. "Is the Technology Revolution Over?" *International Productivity Monitor*, no. 25, pp. 20-36.

Caballero, Ricardo J. 2006. "On the Macroeconomics of Asset Shortages." *NBER Working Paper*, 12753.

____ 2010. "The "Other" Imbalance and the Financial Crisis." *NBER Working Paper*, 15636. Campbell, John Y., Robert J. Shiller, and Luis M. Viceira. 2009. "Understanding Inflation-Indexed Bond Markets." *Brookings Papers on Economic Activity*, Spring, 79- 120.

Campbell, John Y., Adi Sunderam, and Luis M. Viceira. 2013. "Inflation Bets or Deflation Hedges? The Changing Risks of Nominal Bonds." Harvard Business School Working Paper 09-088.

Carroll, Christopher D. and Andrew A. Samwick. 1997. "The Nature of Precautionary Wealth." *Journal of Monetary Economics*, 40(1), 41-71.

Congressional Budget Office. 2015a. "CBO's Economic Forecasting Record: 2015 Update." February.

____ 2015b. "The Budget and Economic Outlook: 2015 to 2025." January.

Cox, John C., Jonathan E. Ingersoll Jr., and Stephen A. Ross. 1985. "A Theory of the Term Structure of Interest Rates." *Econometrica,* 53(2), 385-408.

D'Amico, Stefania, Don H. Kim, and Min Wei. 2014. "Tips from TIPS: the informational Content of Treasury Inflation-Protected Security prices." *Finance and Economics Discussion Series (FEDS) Working Paper*, 2014-24.

David, Paul A. and Gavin Wright. 2006. "General Purpose Technologies and Surges in Productivity: Historical Reflections on the Future of the ICT Revolution." In Paul A. David and Mark Thomas, eds., *The Economic Future in Historical Perspective*, Oxford University Press, Oxford, UK.

Favero, Carlo A., Arie E. Gozluklu, and Haoxi Yang. 2013. "Demographics and the Behavior of Interest Rates." Warwick Business School, Finance Group Working Paper.

Federal Reserve Bank of Philadelphia. "Survey of Professional Forecasters". *Real Time Data Center.* Accessed: June 10, 2015. https://www.philadelphiafed.org/research-and-data/real-time-center/survey-of-professional-forecasters/.

Federal Reserve Board. "Appropriate pace of policy firming: Midpoint of target range or target level for the federal funds rate." *Federal Open Market Committee, June 17 Meeting Projection Materials,* June 17, 2015. http://www.federalreserve.gov/monetarypolicy/files/fomcprojtabl20150617.pdf.

Fernald, John G. 2014. "Productivity and Potential Output before, during, and after the Great Recession" Federal Reserve Bank of San Francisco Working Paper Series.

Fisher, Irving. 1930. *The Theory of Interest*, Macmillan, New York.

Frederick, Shane, George Loewenstein, and Ted O'Donoghue. 2002. "Time Discounting and Time Preference: A Critical Review." *Journal of Economic Literature*, 40(2), 351- 401.

Geanakoplos, John, Michael Magill, and Martine Quinzii. 2004. "Demography and the Long-Run Predictability of the Stock Market." *Brookings Papers on Economic Activity,* Spring, 241-322.

Gordon, Robert J. 2010. "Revisiting U.S. Productivity Growth over the Past Century with a View of the Future." *NBER Working Paper,* 15834.

____ 2014. "A New Method of Estimating Potential Real GDP Growth: Implications for the Labor Market and the Debt/GDP Ratio." *NBER Working Paper,* 20423.

Gourinchas, Pierre-Olivier and Jonathan A. Parker. 2002. "Consumption over the Life Cycle." *Econometrica*, 70(1), 47-89.

Gürkaynak, Refet S, Brian Sack, and Eric Swanson. 2005. "Do Actions Speak Louder than Words? The Response of Asset Prices to Monetary Policy Actions and Statements," *International Journal of Central Banking*, 1(1), 55-93.

Hamilton, James D., Ethan S. Harris, Jan Hatzius and Kenneth D. West. 2015. "The Equilibrium Real Funds Rate: Past, Present, and Future," Working Paper.

Hanson, Samuel G. and Jeremy C. Stein. 2012. "Monetary Policy and Long-Term Real Rates." *Finance and Economics Discussions Series (FEDS) Working Paper No. 2012- 46.* Homer, Sidney and Richard Sylla. 2005. *A History of Interest Rates*, Wiley Press, New York. International Monetary Fund. 2010. *World Economic Outlook.* April.

____ 2014. *World Economic Outlook.* April.

Kahn, James and Robert Rich. 2011. "The Productivity Slowdown Reaffirmed." *Liberty Street Economics.* Federal Reserve Bank of New York.

Kharas, Homi. 2010. "The Emerging Middle Class in Developing Countries." *Working Paper No. 285.* OECD Development Centre, January.

Kim, Don H. and Jonathan H. Wright. 2005. "An Arbitrage-Free Three-Factor Term Structure Model and the Recent Behavior of Long-Term Yields and Distant-Horizon Forward Rates." *Finance and Economics Discussion Series (FEDS) Working Paper,* No. 2005-33.

Krishnamurthy, Arvind and Annette Vissing-Jorgensen. 2011. "The Effects of Quantitative Easing on Long-term Interest Rates." *Brookings Papers on Economic Activity*, Fall, 215-265.

____ 2012. "The Aggregate Demand for Treasury Debt." *Journal of Political Economy,* 120(2), 233-267.

Lawrance, Emily C. 1991. "Poverty and the Rate of Time Preference: Evidence from Panel Data," *Journal of Political Economy,* 99 (1), 54–77.

Li, Canlin and Min Wei. 2013. "Term Structure Modeling with Supply Factors and the Federal Reserve's Large Scale Asset Purchase Programs," *International Journal of Central Banking*, 9(1), 3-39.

Macroeconomic Advisers. 2015. "June 2015 Base Solution File". *Macroeconomic Advisers Model of the U.S. Economy.*

McKinsey Global Institute. 2010. *Farewell to Cheap Capital? The Implications of Long-Term Shifts in Global Investment and Saving.* December. At: http://www.mckinsey.com/insights/global_capital_markets/farewell_cheap_capital.

Mokyr, Joel. 2014. "Ideas, Progress, Wealth, and the Biological Revolution." *The Biologist's Imagination: Innovation in the Biosciences*, 1.

Moore, Michael J. and W. Kip Viscusi. 1990. "Models for Estimating Discount Rates for Long-Term

Health Risks Using Labor Market Data." *Journal of Risk and Uncertainty*, 3, 381- 401.

Neely, Christopher J. and David E. Rapach. 2008. "Real Interest Rate Persistence: Evidence and Implications." *Federal Reserve Bank of St. Louis Review*, 90(6), 609- 641.

Newell, Richard G. and William A. Pizer. 2003. "Discounting the Distant Future: How Much Do Uncertain Rates Increase Valuations?" *Journal of Environmental Economics and Management*, 46(1), 52-71.

Obstfeld, Maurice. 2015. "Trilemmas and Tradeoffs: Living with Financial Globalization." In Claudio Raddatz, Diego Saravia, and Jaume Ventura, eds., *Global Liquidity, Spillovers to Emerging Markets and Policy Responses,* Central Bank of Chile, Santiago, Chile.

Pritchett, Lant and Lawrence H. Summers. 2014. "Asiaphoria Meets Regression to the Mean." *NBER Working Paper,* 20573.

Ramsey, F.P. 1928. "A Mathematical Theory of Saving." *Economic Journal*, 38 (152), 543-559. Reinhart, Carmen and Kenneth Rogoff. 2009. *This Time is Different: Eight Centuries of Financial Folly,* Princeton University Press, Princeton.

Rogoff, Kenneth. 2015. "Debt Supercycle, Not Secular Stagnation." *Vox: CEPR's Policy Portal*, April 22. At: http://www.voxeu.org/article/debt-supercycle-not-secular-stagnation.

Romer, Christina D. and David H. Romer. 2015. "New Evidence on the Impact of Financial Crises in Advanced Countries." *NBER Working Paper,* 21021.

Rose, Andrew K. 1988. "Is the Real Interest Rate Stable?" *Journal of Finance*, 43(5), 1095-1112.

Rudebusch, Glenn D. and Eric T. Swanson. 2012. “The Bond Premium in a DSGE Model with Long- Run Real and Nominal Risks.” *American Economic Journal: Macroeconomics*, 4(1), 105-43. Ruderman, Henry, Mark D. Levine, and James E. McMahon. 1987. "The Behavior of the Market for Energy Efficiency in Residential Appliances Including Heating and Cooling Equipment." *Energy Journal*, 8(1), 101-24.

Shiller, Robert J. 2000. *Irrational Exuberance*. Princeton University Press, Princeton.

____ 2013. “U.S. Stock Price Data, Annual, with consumption, both short and long rates, and present value calculations”. *Online Data Robert Shiller*. Accessed: June 10, 2015. http://www.econ.yale.edu/~shiller/data.htm.

Social Security Administration. 2014. "The 2014 Annual Report of the Board of Trustees of the Federal Old-Age and Survivors Insurance and Federal Disability Insurance Trust Funds." http://www.ssa.gov/oact/tr/2014/index.html

Stock, James H. and Mark W. Watson. 2003. “Has the Business Cycle Changed and Why?” In Kenneth Rogoff and Mark Gertler, eds., NBER *Macroeconomics Annual 2002*, 17, 159-230. Summers, Lawrence H. 2014. “Reflections on the ‘New Secular Stagnation Hypothesis’.” In Coen Teulings and Richard Baldwin, eds., *Secular Stagnation: Facts, Causes and Cures*. London, UK: Centre for Economic Policy Research.

Thornton, Daniel L. and Giorgio Valente. 2012. “Out-of-Sample Predictions of Bond Excess Returns and Forward Rates: An Asset Allocation Perspective.” *Review of Financial Studies*, 25(10), 3141-68.

Warren, George F., and Frank Pearson. 1935. “Gold and Prices.” *Wiley and Sons*. New York.

Weitzman, Martin L. 2009. “On Modeling and Interpreting the Economics of Catastrophic Climate Change.” *Review of Economics and Statistics,* 91(1), 1-19.

APPENDICES

Appendix A: Infinite Horizon Growth Model with Labor-Augmenting Technical Progress

Consider a representative household that makes optimal consumption plans over an infinite horizon. The instantaneous utility function of an individual at date *t* is given by:

(1) $$u(c_t)$$

where c_t is consumption per worker. We assume that $u(c)$ is strictly increasing, concave, twice continuously differentiable, and satisfies the following Inada conditions:

$$\lim_{c\to 0} u'(c) = \infty \text{ and } \lim_{c\to\infty} u'(c) = 0$$

Labor is inelastically supplied to producers. The labor force grows at rate *n*. Without loss of generality, the population at date 0 is normalized to 1 ($L_0 = 1$). At date *t* the size of the labor force is:

(2) $$L_t = (1+n)^t L_0$$

The economy experiences exogenous labor-augmenting technical progress at rate g. Thus, the production function for this economy is

(3) $$Y_t = F[K_t, A_t L_t],$$

Where Y_t is real output and K_t is the capital stock. $A_t L_t$ is the effective labor force where $A_t = (1+g)^t A_0$ and the initial level of technology is again normalized to 1 ($A_0 = 1$).

We assume that the production function has constant returns to scale, and this allows us to rescale and simplify this equation by expressing output per unit of effective labor as a function of capital per effective labor:

$$\hat{y}_t \equiv \frac{Y_t}{A_t L_t} \equiv F\left[\frac{K_t}{A_t L_t}, 1\right] \equiv f(\hat{k}_t)$$

where a "hat" over a variable expresses it as a ratio to the number of effective workers, $A_t L_t$.

Characterizing the balanced growth path:

Assume that the utility function is of the constant relative risk aversion (CRRA) class:

(4) $$U(c) = \begin{cases} \frac{c^{1-\sigma}-1}{1-\sigma} if & \sigma \neq 1 \, and \, \sigma \geq 0 \\ \ln c \;\; if \; \sigma = 1 \end{cases}$$

The coefficient of relative risk aversion is σ:

$$\sigma = -\frac{u''(c_t)c_t}{u'(c_t)}$$

The inverse of σ is the intertemporal elasticity of substitution. The intertemporal elasticity of substitution, $1/\sigma$, measures the extent to which households are willing to substitute consumption today for consumption tomorrow, taking into account diminishing marginal utility.[32] How an individual values utility in different years is governed by the subjective discount factor, β, in the equation below.

The stream of utility for the economy as whole is given by the sum of period utilities, discounted by $\beta < 1$:

$$U_0 \equiv \sum_{t=0}^{\infty} \beta^t \, L_t u(c_t)$$

The utility function can be transformed into per effective worker units by adjusting the effective discount factor to reflect the rate of population growth and the rate of technical progress:[33] $\beta(1+n)(1+g)^{1-\sigma}$. To ensure that the household's maximization problem has a solution, we assume that $\beta(1+n)(1+g)^{1-\sigma} < 1$.

Along the optimal growth path the representative household chooses a plan for consumption and capital investment to maximize its utility subject to technological and feasibility constraints:

$$\hat{k}_{t+1}(1+n)(1+g) - \hat{k}_t = f(\hat{k}_t) - \hat{c}_t$$

For simplicity we assume a zero percent depreciation rate. The current-value Lagrangian for this problem is:

$$L = \sum_{t=0}^{\infty} \beta^t (1+n)^t (1+g)^{(1-\sigma)t} \{U(\hat{c}_t) + \mu_t [f(\hat{k}_t) - (\hat{k}_{t+1}(1+n)(1+g) - \hat{k}_t) - \hat{c}_t]\}$$

There are an infinite number of optimality conditions which govern allocations for each period t. Below are the first-order conditions derived from differentiating with respect to 1) consumption per effective labor unit at time t, 2) capital per effective labor unit at time t+1, and 3), the Lagrange multiplier at t:

$$u'(\hat{c}_t) = \mu_t$$

$$\beta^t (1+n)^t (1+g)^{(1-\sigma)t} \mu_t (1+n)(1+g) = \beta^{t+1} (1+n)^{t+1} (1+g)^{(1-\sigma)(t+1)} \mu_{t+1} (f'(\hat{k}_{t+1}) + 1)$$

$$f(\hat{k}_t) - (\hat{k}_{t+1}(1+n)(1+g) - \hat{k}_t) - \hat{c}_t = 0$$

The second first-order condition can be re-arranged to yield

(5) $$\frac{\mu_t}{\mu_{t+1}} = \beta(1+g)^{-\sigma} \left(1 + f'(\hat{k}_{t+1})\right)$$

Along a balanced growth path $\frac{\mu_t}{\mu_{t+1}} = 1$ so

$$1 + f'(\hat{k}_{t+1}) = \frac{1}{\beta}(1+g)^{\sigma}$$

The marginal product of capital per effective labor unit in steady state is a constant, and depends on the rate of time discount, the household's willingness to substitute over time, and the rate of technical progress. Note that the rate of population growth does not affect the steady state interest rate because the household endogenously saves enough for future generations in order to keep the capital:effective labor ratio constant. In the steady state, consumption per worker and output per worker grow at rate g, and aggregate consumption, aggregate output and aggregate capital grow at rate $n+g$.

The problem above was written in discrete time but the Ramsey condition that connects the real interest rate to consumption growth is often expressed in continuous time; that is, the limit of the first order condition as the unit of time goes to zero. Let $\beta = \frac{1}{1+\rho}$ describe the relationship between the discount factor and the discount rate. Further, let the discount factor for a period of length Δ be $\beta(\Delta) = (1+\rho\Delta)^{-\frac{1}{\Delta}}$. As we let Δ go to 0, we have—using the definition of the mathematical constant e –

$$\lim_{\Delta\to 0}\beta(\Delta) = \lim_{\Delta\to 0}(1+\rho\Delta)^{-\frac{1}{\Delta}} = e^{-\rho}$$

as our continuous discount factor. Applying this logic to the expression for the marginal product of capital we have:

$$1 + f'\left(\hat{k}_{(t+1)}\right) = (1+\rho)(1+g)^{\sigma}$$

$$\left[1 + f'\left(\hat{k}_{(t+1+\Delta)}\right)\Delta\right]^{\frac{1}{\Delta}} \approx (1+\rho\Delta)^{\frac{1}{\Delta}}(1+g\Delta)^{\frac{1}{\Delta}\sigma}$$

Taking the limit as $\Delta \to 0$, we have

$$exp\left[f'\left(\hat{k}_t\right)\right] = \exp(\rho)\exp(\sigma g),$$

or

$$f'\left(\hat{k}_t\right) = \rho + \sigma g,$$

which is the solution for the continuous time case, and which appears as equation (2) in the main text.

Appendix B: Long-Term Interest Rate and Term Premium

Adding uncertainty to the previous model leads to a theory of long-term real and nominal interest rates. An obvious candidate for the role of random shocks is the productivity factor A_t, although the analysis that follows is applicable even when there are further sources of uncertainty (for example, in household preferences). Now, if $E_t\{\cdot\}$ denotes a mathematical expectation conditional on date-t information, the representative household maximizes the *expected value* of lifetime utility, given by

$$U_0 \equiv E_0\left\{\sum_{t=0}^{\infty} \beta^t L_t U(c_t)\right\}$$

In an environment with uncertainty, the first-order condition analogous to equation (5) above, now written in terms of per capita consumption c_t (rather than consumption per effective labor unit $\hat{c}_t$), takes the form

(6) $$u'(c_t) = E_t\left\{\beta u'(c_{t+1})\left(1 + f'\left(\hat{k}_{t+1}\right)\right)\right\}$$

From this condition we can derive the pricing of both long-term real bonds (bonds that are indexed to consumption) and long-term nominal bonds (bonds with money payouts). These results immediately yield formulas for long-term interest rates, which are inversely related to bond prices.

Long-term real interest rates. If the marginal product of date *t*+1 capital, $f'(\hat{k}_{t+1})$, were completely predictable (for example, the technology is non-stochastic and the date t+1 capital stock is fully known on date *t*), then equation (6) above can be re-written as

$$u'(c_t) = \left(1 + f'(\hat{k}_{t+1})\right) E_t\{\beta u'(c_{t+1})\}$$

If the (one-period, net) real interest rate between periods *t* and *t*+1 is denoted by r_{t+1}^1, then investing in a one-period bond is equivalent to investing in (risk-free) capital, and so the preceding first-order condition would imply that

$$u'(c_t) = (1 + r_{t+1}^1) E_t\{\beta u'(c_{t+1})\}$$

A risk-free real (that is, consumption-indexed) one-period bond pays an investor one unit of the consumption good after a period and its date *t* price p_t^1 (measured in terms of consumption) is related to the real interest rate between periods *t* and *t*+1 by

$$p_t^1 = \frac{1}{1 + r_{t+1}^1} = E_t\left\{\frac{\beta u'(c_{t+1})}{u'(c_t)}\right\}$$

This formula states that the date-*t* price of a one-period bond is the expected value of a stochastic discount factor (SDF), $M_{t+1} \equiv \beta u'(c_{t+1})/u'(c_t)$, that gives the ex post date-*t*+1 marginal utility value, relative to today's marginal utility, of a unit of the consumption good delivered on date *t*+1.

This same pricing principle enables one to price bonds with longer maturities, and from those prices, derive long-term interest rates. A *k*-period (pure discount) bond pays an investor one unit of consumption after *k* periods, so its price in terms of consumption on date *t* will be

$$p_t^k = \frac{1}{\left(1 + r_{t+k}^k\right)^k} = E_t\left\{\frac{\beta^k u'(c_{t+k})}{u'(c_t)}\right\},$$

where r_{t+k}^k denotes the *annualized* interest rate on a *k*-period bond that is purchased on date *t* and matures *k* periods later—for short, the *long-term* (*k*-period) real interest rate.

Relation between long and short rates. To understand better the relationship between long- and short-term (one-period) rates of interest, define the date-*t*+*j* SDF by $M_{t+j} \equiv \beta u'(c_{t+j})/u'(c_{t+j-1})$. In terms of this more compact notation, the price of a *k*-period bond is

$$p_t^k = E_t\{M_{t+1} M_{t+2} \dots M_{t+k}\}$$

The law of iterated conditional expectations implies that the preceding bond price also has the representation (see also Rudebusch and Swanson 2012):

(7) $p_t^k = E_t\{E_{t+1}\{M_{t+1}M_{t+2} \dots M_{t+k}\}\} = E_t\{M_{t+1}E_{t+1}\{M_{t+2} \dots M_{t+k}\}\} = E_t\{M_{t+1}p_{t+1}^{k-1}\},$

where p_{t+1}^{k-1} is the date-t+1 price of a bond maturing after $k-1$ periods.

If $Cov_t\{\cdot\}$ denotes conditional covariance, then this expression further reduces to:

$$p_t^k = E_t\{M_{t+1}\}E_t\{p_{t+1}^{k-1}\} + Cov_t\{M_{t+1}, p_{t+1}^{k-1}\}$$

But repetition of the earlier argument, in the case of a k-1 period bond traded on date t+1, shows that

$$p_{t+1}^{k-1} = E_{t+1}\{M_{t+2}p_{t+2}^{k-2}\},$$

so that

$$E_t\{p_{t+1}^{k-1}\} = E_t\{M_{t+2}p_{t+2}^{k-2}\} = E_t\{M_{t+2}\}E_t\{p_{t+2}^{k-2}\} + Cov_t\{M_{t+2}, p_{t+2}^{k-2}\}$$

Substituting this expression above into the last equation for p_t^k, recalling the relation between the short-term real interest rate and the SDF, and iterating, gives:

$$p_t^k = \prod_{j=1}^{k} E_t\{M_{t+j}\} + \sum_{j=1}^{k-1}\left(\prod_{h=1}^{j-1} E_t\{M_{t+h}\}\right) Cov_t\{M_{t+j}, p_{t+j}^{k-j}\}$$

$$= \prod_{j=1}^{k} E_t\left\{\frac{1}{1+r_{t+j}^1}\right\} + \sum_{j=1}^{k-1}\left(\prod_{h=1}^{j-1} E_t\left\{\frac{1}{1+r_{t+h}^1}\right\}\right) Cov_t\{M_{t+j}, p_{t+j}^{k-j}\}$$

Finally, this last result shows that the long-term k-period interest rate is given by

$$\frac{1}{\left(1+r_{t+k}^k\right)^k} = \prod_{j=1}^{k} E_t\left\{\frac{1}{1+r_{t+j}^1}\right\} + \sum_{j=1}^{k-1}\left(\prod_{h=1}^{j-1} E_t\left\{\frac{1}{1+r_{t+h}^1}\right\}\right) Cov_t\{M_{t+j}, p_{t+j}^{k-j}\}$$

Absent the second term on the right-hand side above, the k-period discount factor would just be the product of expected future one-period discount factors—a statement of the "expectations theory" of the term structure, according to which the return from investing in a k-period bond is closely related to the expected return from investing in a sequence of k one-period bonds. The second right-hand term, however, is a risk premium which arises because on every date, the investor might wish to liquidate rather than continue holding the long-term bond. After j periods have elapsed, the k-period bond is a $(k-j)$-period bond. If the price of a $(k-j)$-period bond tends to be high when the growth rate of the marginal utility of consumption M_{t+j} is high, for example, this results in a positive value of $Cov_t\{M_{t+j}, p_{t+j}^{k-j}\}$, which lowers the long-term interest rate r_{t+k}^k, other things equal. In this case, the period $t+j$ contribution to the risk premium is negative, because the statistical tendency of bond-price movement for that maturity provides consumption insurance, being positive when consumption falls. Under the opposite covariance assumption, the bond raises the riskiness of consumption, contributing to a higher value of the long-term interest rate. In total, the risk premium depends on the discounted sum of covariances of the bond price (over its remaining maturity) with consumption growth on every date until the bond matures.

Approximate solutions. A somewhat simpler but approximate version of the long-term interest rate formula is available under the assumption that future SDFs follow a lognormal statistical distribution (in which case bond prices also will be lognormally distributed). Let $m_{t+j} \equiv lnM_{t+j}$. Then m_{t+j} follows a normal distribution and equation (7) above takes the form

$$ln(p_t^k) = E_t\{m_{t+1}\} + E_t\{ln(p_{t+1}^{k-1})\} + Cov_t\{m_{t+1}, ln(p_{t+1}^{k-1})\} + \tfrac{1}{2}Var_t\{m_{t+1}\} + \tfrac{1}{2}Var_t\{ln(p_{t+1}^{k-1})\}$$

($Var_t\{\cdot\}$ denotes a conditional variance.) An iterative procedure analogous to the one followed before, starting by eliminating $E_t\{lnp_{t+1}^{k-1}\}$ on the right-hand side above, leads to

$$ln(p_t^k) = \sum_{j=1}^{k} E_t\{m_{t+j}\} + \sum_{j=1}^{k-1} Cov_t\{m_{t+j}, ln(p_{t+j}^{k-j})\} + convexity\ terms$$

Next we express this relation in terms of the approximations $r_{t+k}^k \approx -\frac{1}{k}ln(p_t^k)$ and, for short-term interest rates, $r_{t+j}^1 \approx -E_t\{m_{t+j}\} - \frac{1}{2}Var_t\{ln(m_{t+1})\}$. The result, again assuming CRRA/isoelastic utility, is

(8) $$r_{t+k}^k \approx \tfrac{1}{k}\textstyle\sum_{j=1}^{k} E_t\{r_{t+j}^1\} + \tfrac{\sigma}{k}\textstyle\sum_{j=1}^{k-1} Cov_t\{ln(c_{t+j}) - ln(c_{t+j-1}), ln(p_{t+j}^{k-j})\} + convexity\ terms$$

The first summation above shows that the long-term interest rate depends on the average of expected future short-term rates over the life of the long-term bond. The second shows that the long-term rate on a bond also depends on whether, on average, the bond's residual value is positively or negatively correlated with consumption growth. In the former case, the bond is a bad hedge for consumption risk and individuals will demand a return premium to the long-term bond rather than rolling over a succession of one-period bonds. In the latter case, the risk premium embedded in the long-term rate of interest is, instead, negative.

Nominal long-term interest rates. The previous analysis considered a *real* bond, such as TIPS, whose payouts are indexed to the CPI. Similar principles apply, however, to the pricing of *nominal* bonds, which have money payoffs. The main difference is that expectations about inflation—the rate of increase of the price level—play a role in pricing long-term nominal bonds and hence in determining long-term nominal interest rates (interest rates on loans of money that are not somehow indexed to the price level).[34]

The stochastic discount factor in this case reflects the relative future marginal consumption value of a money payment and if P_t denotes the general price level, the former is

$$N_{t+j} = \frac{\beta u'(c_{t+j})/P_{t+j}}{u'(c_{t+j-1})/P_{t+j-1}}$$

The one-period nominal interest rate on date t, denoted i_{t+1}^1, satisfies

$$\frac{1}{1+i_{t+1}^1} = E_t\{N_{t+1}\}$$

Moreover, through reasoning similar to that above, the price (in terms of money) of a k-period nominal bond on date t, denoted by q_t^k, obeys the pricing formula

$$q_t^k = E_t\{N_{t+1}q_{t+1}^{k-1}\},$$

which is parallel to equation (7) above. All the steps taken above to draw implication from equation (7) therefore have exact analogs in the case of nominal bonds.

To get more quickly to a practicable formula for the long-term nominal interest rate, define the (approximate) inflation rate as $\pi_{t+1} = lnP_{t+1} - ln\,P_t$; note another important approximation, the famous Fisher (1930) equation linking the nominal interest rate to the short-term real interest rate and the expected rate of inflation,

$$i_{t+1}^1 = r_{t+1}^1 + E_t\{\pi_{t+1}\};$$

and observe that for CRRA/isoelastic utility, $lnN_{t+1} = -\sigma\left(ln(c_{t+j}) - ln(c_{t+j-1})\right) - \pi_{t+j}$. These results lead to an approximation for the long-term nominal rate of interest that parallels equation (8) above:

$$i_{t+k}^k \approx \frac{1}{k}\sum_{j=1}^{k} E_t\{r_{t+j}^1 + \pi_{t+j}\} + \frac{1}{k}\sum_{j=1}^{k-1} Cov_t\{\sigma[ln(c_{t+j}) - ln(c_{t+j-1})] + \pi_{t+j}, ln(q_{t+j}^{k-j})\}$$

$$+\ convexity\ terms$$

As noted in the text, the nominal long-term interest rate depends positively on:

1. Expected future short term real interest rates.
2. Expected future inflation rates.
3. The extent to which bond prices tend to vary positively with consumption growth.
4. The extent to which bond prices tend to vary positively with inflation (because the bond has a high value when the value of money is low, which makes it less valuable as a hedge).

Items (1) and (2) above correspond to a pure expectations theory of the term structure. Items (3) and (4) above sum to the risk premium in the long-term nominal interest rate.

Appendix C: Relationship between TFP and Labor Productivity

Assume that production is Cobb-Douglas with α equal to capital's share in national income, which will be constant along a balanced growth path. Labor productivity (output per person) grows at the rate *g*:

(9) $$\%\Delta(Y/L) = \alpha\ \%\Delta\ (K/L) + (1\text{-}\alpha)\ \%\Delta(A) = g$$

Total factor productivity (output less factor inputs) is equal to the labor share times *g*:

(10) $$\%\Delta(Y) - \alpha\ \%\Delta\ (K) - (1-\ \alpha)\ \%\Delta(L) = \ (1-\ \alpha)\ g$$

Appendix D: International Interest-Rate Linkages and Exchange Rates

Countries' nominal bonds are usually denominated in different national currencies, which means that investors comparing the rates of return available in different national bond markets must consider how exchange rates might move over the life of an investment. In a hypothetical world with no uncertainty, where investors have perfect foresight of the future, arbitrage in financially integrated markets would imply that any bond must yield the same amount of currency upon maturity. Thus, if i is the nominal interest rate on a domestic-currency nominal bond, i^* the nominal interest rate on a foreign-currency bond, and e the rate at which the home currency is expected to lose value against foreign currency in the foreign exchange market (the rate of depreciation of domestic against foreign currency), then

$$i = i^* + e$$

This *nominal interest-rate parity* condition states that in equilibrium, all bonds offer the same yield when yields are measured in the same currency.

According to Fisher (1930), if π is the domestic expected inflation rate, the real interest rate on a domestic bond is given by $r = i - \pi$, with a parallel expression in the foreign country based on the foreign expected inflation rate π^*. With these definitions, upon subtracting π from both sides of the preceding nominal interest-rate parity condition, one arrives at the *real interest-rate* parity condition that ties together different economies; real rates of interest:

$$r = r^* + (e + \pi^* - \pi)$$

The second term $e + \pi^* - \pi$ on the right-hand side above is the expected change in the *real* or inflation-adjusted exchange rate, which measures the real purchasing power of foreign currency in terms of domestic currency. Because empirically speaking, long-term changes in real exchange rates are very hard to predict apart from slow-moving trends based on demographics and productivity, there will be a strong tendency for long-run national real interest rates to move together in a financially integrated world (though possibly with relatively slowly moving gaps between the levels). If long-run central bank inflation targets are steady, different countries long-run nominal interest rates will inherit a similar tendency to move together.

Once realistic uncertainty about the future is recognized, the preceding interest-parity relationships must be augmented with appropriate risk premiums. Particularly at long maturities, common shocks to global bond prices (for example, due to global growth expectations or movements in global risk aversion), are likely to reinforce rather than offset the tendency for long-run interest rates to move in a synchronized fashion.

End Notes

[1] Bond yield data are taken from the website of Robert Shiller, at http://www.econ.yale.edu/~shiller/data.htm, under "long term stock, bond, interest rate and consumption data" (http://www.econ.yale.edu/~shiller/data/chapt26.xls). Historical bond yields are also available from the National Bureau of Economic Research Macrohistory database, Chapter 13 (Interest Rates). For the pre-1953 period, Shiller uses yields on 10-year government bonds from Homer (2005). The bond yield is the market yield at constant maturity, quoted on an investment basis.

[2] Inflation expectations are not observable, and, moreover, can differ between individuals. As a result, measurement of the real interest rate based on nominal rates requires some assumption about "the" expected rate of inflation. In this report we therefore use alternative measures as a check on sensitivity.

[3] Because investors in nominal bonds are concerned about their future real purchasing power, the inflation rate relevant for pricing those bonds is the change in the PCE deflator, which is closer to an ideal index of money's purchasing power than is the fixed-weight Consumer Price Index (CPI). In Figure 2, however, we use the year-over- year percent change in the annual CPI, because it is available back to 1871. The CPI-U (Consumer Price Index-All Urban Consumers) is reported by the U.S. Bureau of Labor Statistics from 1913. For years before 1913, Shiller splices the CPI-U with Warren and Pearson's price index (Warren and Pearson 1935). For details on how Shiller spliced the two series, see footnote 2 on page 235 of Shiller (2000).

[4] Newell and Pizer (2003) argue that the trend of a declining real interest rate goes back much further than 1876.

[5] SPF expected inflation is the median expected 10-year inflation estimate of the Federal Reserve Bank of Philadelphia's Survey of Professional Forecasters. The median number of forecasters between 1981:Q3 and 1990:Q1 was 21. Since 1990:Q1, the median has been 37.

[6] The real rate is once again measured as the annual rate on the 10-year government bond less the lagged and current 5-year moving average of annual CPI inflation.

[7] The forecasts presented are those reported in the Blue Chip Economic Indicators survey in March of each calendar year, reflecting the average of over 50 professional forecasts. Similar patterns are evident in Administration forecasts reported in the annual *Economic Report of the President*.

[8] The root mean square error is a commonly used measure of the deviation between predicted and actual values. The difference between the two values is squared and then summed over time. The square root of that number is typically reported as a summary statistic, with large values indicating large prediction errors.

[9] A time series is said to contain a unit root if its random changes contain a permanent component. In this case it is statistically non-stationary.

[10] Hamilton et. al. (2015) reject the hypothesis that the real interest rate converges to a fixed constant. The difficulty in predicting the long-run real interest rate leads them to be skeptical of models, like the Ramsey model considered below, that place a strong emphasis on the link between output growth and the real interest rate.

[11] Even when interest rates are mean-reverting, and therefore stationary in the statistical sense, they can be "trend-stationary," reverting to means that evolve deterministically over time rather than being constants. Thus, stationarity of interest rates does not rule out the possibility that they trend upward or downward over long periods as a result of somewhat predictable, secular economic forces.

[12] Under the class of preferences assumed here, the household's attitude to smoothing consumption across time is identical to its attitude toward smoothing across uncertain future states of the world, conflating intertemporal substitutability with risk aversion. Epstein-Zin-Weil preferences are often used to allow for a separation of the desire for smoothing consumption over time from attitudes toward risk.

[13] For a comprehensive review of this literature, see Neely and Rapach (2008).

[14] Some of the studies estimate total factor productivity (TFP), rather than labor productivity, g. Estimated TFP is divided by labor's share of income to obtain g. See Appendix C for the correspondence between labor productivity and total factor productivity.

[15] As presented, equation (3) omits additional convexity terms involving variances, in order to simplify the exposition and highlight the role of covariances in term premiums.

[16] This follows from recalling that, because of the Fisher equation, $E_t\{r^1_{t+j} + \pi_{t+j}\}$ is the expected short-term nominal interest rate on date $t + j - 1$.

[17] Credit risk premiums have appeared in U.S. Treasuries, however, under the threat that Congress might refuse to raise the Federal debt limit, thereby possibly forcing default.

[18] Note here that we are not using the asset pricing framework to "solve" for interest rates, as we did with the Ramsey model. That is possible in principle, but only on the basis of additional and much stronger assumptions than those made above. Rather, we are turning to asset markets to inform us about the likely contributions of the different components to the total return.

[19] See, for example, Gürkaynak, et al. (2005) or Hanson and Stein (2012).

[20] Thornton and Valente compare the excess returns of a bond portfolio based on the information from forward rates with the excess returns on a bond portfolio based on current (no expectations) information. The models based on forward rates fail to outperform the no-predictability benchmark.

[21] As noted above, the theory implies that the consumer wishes to insure against changes in his or her purchasing power, so the personal consumption expenditure deflator, rather than the CPI, would be the more appropriate deflator. The CPI and the PCE deflators are strongly,

though not perfectly correlated; and CPI inflation is typically slightly higher than PCE inflation, on average by about 0.25 percentage point on an annual basis. Because TIPS are indexed to the CPI and not the PCE, their market yield is therefore below the "true" model-implied real interest rate by 0.25 percentage point.

[22] This spread is the average difference between the FOMC rate and the three-month treasury rate based on monthly data between July 1954 and February 2015.

[23] Their method is very similar to that used by Kim and Wright (2005). Kim and Wright use a three-factor model and survey data, which limits the time interval over which the model can be estimated. Adrian et al. (2013) show that their five-factor model, without survey information, comes very close to replicating Kim and Wright and has the advantage of extending back to the 1960s.

[24] Kim and Wright (2005) use inflation data to separate the overall term premium into what they call an inflation term premium and a real term premium. They attribute two-thirds of the decline in the term premium to the real component.

[25] If the Ramsey model is valid, then in the short run that interest rate can be viewed as determining the growth *rate* of per capita consumption through the Ramsey model's Euler equation, with the *level* of per capita consumption adjusting so that saving equals investment. In the long-run balanced growth equilibrium, the long-run growth rate of labor productivity determines the interest rate (while there, too, saving equals investment).

[26] Measures of capital market integration include the correlation between saving and investment rates, correlations between consumption growth rates across countries, the magnitude and responsiveness to return differentials of international capital flows, tests for interest-rate parity, indices of legal impediments to capital movements, and the like.

[27] For more evidence on the close co-movements of different countries' long-term nominal interest rates, see Obstfeld (2015).

[28] The real rate is the annual rate on the 10-year government bond less the lagged and current 5-year moving average of annual CPI inflation.

[29] In International Monetary Fund (2014), the IMF conducted a principal component analysis of the contribution of three common global factors to variations in real interest rates of a group of 17 developed countries. The contribution of the first factor increased roughly 20 percentage points to nearly 75 percent between 1980-1995 and 1996-2012.

[30] The "Ricardian equivalence" hypothesis—that private households will fully internalize and therefore undo the effects of government spending and taxation—rests on the assumptions that households have rational expectations and infinite-horizon dynastic preferences.

[31] While the preceding description fits the very recent experience of the advanced economies as well as other notable episodes (such as Japan after the early 1990s), Romer and Romer (2015) document that financial shocks induce slowdowns of varying depth and persistence in OECD countries, depending on the magnitude and duration of the associated financial distress.

[32] In order to explain macroeconomic phenomena simultaneously with asset prices, many financial models adopt non-standard preferences that allow for a separation of the desire for smoothing consumption over time from attitudes toward risk. When preferences under uncertainty are of the standard expected-utility variety, which makes household welfare a linear function of the probabilities of future uncertain events, the household's attitude to smoothing consumption across time is identical to its attitude toward smoothing across uncertain future states of the world, and so standard intertemporal preferences conflate intertemporal substitutability with risk aversion.

[33] In other words, the growth path of $\beta L_t u(c_t)$ is equal to the growth path of $\beta(1+n)(1+g)^{1-\sigma}u(\hat{c}_t)$. Since additive constant terms in objective functions do not affect optimal decisions, the term –1 in the utility function is omitted when making the transformation in utility from per worker to per effective worker units.

[34] As noted above, the PCE, not the CPI, is the more relevant index of the purchasing power of money for modeling nominal bond prices and nominal interest rates.

In: Long Term Interest Rates
Editor: Daryl Watkins

ISBN: 978-1-63483-747-7

Chapter 2

THE GLOBAL SAVING GLUT AND THE U.S. CURRENT ACCOUNT DEFICIT*

Ben S. Bernanke

On most dimensions the U.S. economy appears to be performing well. Output growth has returned to healthy levels, the labor market is firming, and inflation appears to be well controlled. However, one aspect of U.S. economic performance still evokes concern among economists and policymakers: the nation's large and growing current account deficit. In the first three quarters of 2004, the U.S. external deficit stood at $635 billion at an annual rate, or about 5-1/2 percent of the U.S. gross domestic product (GDP). Corresponding to that deficit, U.S. citizens, businesses, and governments on net had to raise $635 billion on international capital markets.[1] The current account deficit has been on a steep upward trajectory in recent years, rising from a relatively modest $120 billion (1.5 percent of GDP) in 1996 to $414 billion (4.2 percent of GDP) in 2000 on its way to its current level. Most forecasters expect the nation's current account imbalance to decline slowly at best, implying a continued need for foreign credit and a concomitant decline in the U.S. net foreign asset position.

Why is the United States, with the world's largest economy, borrowing heavily on international capital markets–rather than lending, as would seem

* This is an edited, reformatted and augmented version of a speech presented by Federal Reserve Board Governor Bernanke at the Sandridge Lecture, Virginia Association of Economists, Richmond, Virginia, March 10, 2005.

more natural? What implications do the U.S. current account deficit and our consequent reliance on foreign credit have for economic performance in the United States and in our trading partners? What policies, if any, should be used to address this situation? In my remarks today I will offer some tentative answers to these questions. My answers will be somewhat unconventional in that I will take issue with the common view that the recent deterioration in the U.S. current account *primarily* reflects economic policies and other economic developments within the United States itself. Although domestic developments have certainly played a role, I will argue that a satisfying explanation of the recent upward climb of the U.S. current account deficit requires a global perspective that more fully takes into account events outside the United States. To be more specific, I will argue that over the past decade a combination of diverse forces has created a significant increase in the global supply of saving–a global saving glut–which helps to explain both the increase in the U.S. current account deficit and the relatively low level of long-term real interest rates in the world today. The prospect of dramatic increases in the ratio of retirees to workers in a number of major industrial economies is one important reason for the high level of global saving. However, as I will discuss, a particularly interesting aspect of the global saving glut has been a remarkable reversal in the flows of credit to developing and emerging-market economies, a shift that has transformed those economies from borrowers on international capital markets to large net lenders.

To be clear, in locating the principal causes of the U.S. current account deficit outside the country's borders, I am not making a value judgment about the behavior of either U.S. or foreign residents or their governments. Rather, I believe that understanding the influence of global factors on the U.S. current account deficit is essential for understanding the effects of the deficit and for devising policies to address it. Of course, as always, the views I express today are not necessarily shared by my colleagues at the Federal Reserve.[2]

The U.S. Current Account Deficit: Two Perspectives

We will find it helpful to consider, as background for the analysis of the U.S. current account deficit, two alternative ways of thinking about the phenomenon–one that relates the deficit to the patterns of U.S. trade and a second that focuses on saving, investment, and international financial flows.

Although these two ways of viewing the current account derive from accounting identities and thus are ultimately two sides of the same coin, each provides a useful lens for examining the issue.

The first perspective on the current account focuses on patterns of international trade. You are probably aware that the United States has been experiencing a substantial trade imbalance in recent years, with U.S. imports of goods and services from abroad outstripping U.S. exports to other countries by a wide margin. According to preliminary data, in 2004 the United States imported $1.76 trillion worth of goods and services while exporting goods and services valued at only $1.15 trillion. Reflecting this imbalance in trade, current payments from U.S. residents to foreigners (consisting primarily of our spending on imports, but also including certain other types of payments, such as remittances, interest, and dividends) greatly exceed the analogous payments that U.S. residents receive from abroad. By definition, this excess of U.S. payments to foreigners over payments received in a given period equals the U.S. current account deficit, which, as I have already noted, was on track to equal $635 billion in 2004–close to the $618 billion by which the value of U.S. imports exceeded that of exports.

When U.S. receipts from its sales of exports and other current payments are insufficient to cover the cost of U.S. imports and other payments to foreigners, U.S. households, firms, and governments on net must borrow the difference on international capital markets.[3] Thus, essentially by definition, in each period U.S. net foreign borrowing equals the U.S. current account deficit, which in turn is closely linked to the imbalance in U.S. international trade.

That the nation's imports currently far exceed its exports is both widely understood and of concern to many Americans, particularly those whose livelihoods depend on the viability of exporting and import-competing industries. The extensive attention paid to the trade imbalance in the media and elsewhere has tempted some observers to ascribe the growing current account deficit to factors such as changes in the quality or composition of U.S. and foreign-made products, changes in trade policy, or unfair foreign competition. However, I believe–and I suspect that most economists would agree–that specific trade-related factors cannot explain either the magnitude of the U.S. current account imbalance or its recent sharp rise. Rather, the U.S. trade balance is the tail of the dog; for the most part, it has been passively determined by foreign and domestic incomes, asset prices, interest rates, and exchange rates, which are themselves the products of more fundamental driving forces. Instead, an alternative perspective on the current account appears likely to be more useful for explaining recent developments. This second perspective focuses on international financial flows and the basic fact that, within each country, saving and investment need not be equal in each period.

In the United States, as in all countries, economic growth requires investment in new capital goods and the upgrading and replacement of older capital. Examples of capital investment include the construction of factories and office buildings and firms' acquisition of new equipment, ranging from drill presses to computers to airplanes. Residential construction–the building of new homes and apartment buildings–is also counted as part of capital investment.[4]

All investment in new capital goods must be financed in some manner. In a closed economy without trade or international capital flows, the funding for investment would be provided entirely by the country's national saving. By definition, national saving is the sum of saving done by households (for example, through contributions to employer-sponsored 401k accounts) and saving done by businesses (in the form of retained earnings) less any budget deficit run by the government (which is a use rather than a source of saving)[5].

As I say, in a closed economy investment would equal national saving in each period; but, in fact, virtually all economies today are open economies, and well-developed international capital markets allow savers to lend to those who wish to make capital investments in any country, not just their own. Because saving can cross international borders, a country's domestic investment in new capital and its domestic saving need not be equal in each period. If a country's saving exceeds its investment during a particular year, the difference represents excess saving that can be lent on international capital markets. By the same token, if a country's saving is less than the amount required to finance domestic investment, the country can close the gap by borrowing from abroad. In the United States, national saving is currently quite low and falls considerably short of U.S. capital investment. Of necessity, this shortfall is made up by net foreign borrowing–essentially, by making use of foreigners' saving to finance part of domestic investment. We saw earlier that the current account deficit equals the net amount that the United States borrows abroad in each period, and I have just shown that U.S. net foreign borrowing equals the excess of U.S. capital investment over U.S. national saving. It follows that the country's current account deficit equals the excess of its investment over its saving.

To summarize, I have described two equivalent ways of interpreting the current account deficit, one in terms of trade flows and related payments and one in terms of investment and national saving. In general, the perspective one takes depends on the particular analysis at hand.

As I have already suggested, most economists who have offered explanations of the high and rising level of the U.S. current account deficit and the country's foreign borrowing have emphasized investment-saving behavior rather than trade-related factors (and I will do the same today). Along these lines, one commonly hears that the U.S. current account deficit is the product of a precipitous decline in the U.S. national saving rate, which in recent years has fallen to a level that is far from adequate to fund domestic investment. For example, in 1985 U.S. gross national saving was 18 percent of GDP, and in 1995 it was 16 percent of GDP; in 2004, by contrast, U.S. national saving was less than 14 percent of GDP. Those who emphasize the role of low U.S. saving often go on to conclude that, for the most part, the U.S. current account deficit is "made in the U.S.A." and is independent (to a first approximation) of developments in other parts of the globe.

That inadequate U.S. national saving is the source of the current account deficit must be true at some level; indeed, the statement is almost a tautology. However, linking current-account developments to the decline in saving begs the question of *why* U.S. saving has declined. In particular, although the decline in U.S. saving may reflect changes in household behavior or economic policy in the United States, it may also be in some part a reaction to events external to the United States–a hypothesis that I will propose and defend momentarily.

One popular argument for the "made in the U.S.A." explanation of declining national saving and the rising current account deficit focuses on the burgeoning U.S. federal budget deficit, which in 2004 drained more than $400 billion from the national saving pool. I will discuss the link between the budget deficit and the current account deficit in more detail later. Here I simply note that the so-called twin-deficits hypothesis, that government budget deficits cause current account deficits, does not account for the fact that the U.S. external deficit expanded by about $300 billion between 1996 and 2000, a period during which the federal budget was in surplus and projected to remain so. Nor, for that matter, does the twin-deficits hypothesis shed any light on why a number of major countries, including Germany and Japan, continue to run large current account *surpluses* despite government budget deficits that are similar in size (as a share of GDP) to that of the United States. It seems unlikely, therefore, that changes in the U.S. government budget position can entirely explain the behavior of the U.S. current account over the past decade.

The Changing Pattern of International Capital Flows and the Global Saving Glut

What then accounts for the rapid increase in the U.S. current account deficit? My own preferred explanation focuses on what I see as the emergence of a global saving glut in the past eight to ten years. This saving glut is the result of a number of developments. As I will discuss in more detail later, one well-understood source of the saving glut is the strong saving motive of rich countries with aging populations, which must make provision for an impending sharp increase in the number of retirees relative to the number of workers. With slowly growing or declining workforces, as well as high capital-labor ratios, many advanced economies outside the United States also face an apparent dearth of domestic investment opportunities. As a consequence of high desired saving and the low prospective returns to domestic investment, the mature industrial economies as a group seek to run current account surpluses and thus to lend abroad.[6]

Although strong saving motives on the part of many industrial economies contribute to the global saving glut, the saving behavior of these countries does not explain much of the *increase* in desired global saving in the past decade. Indeed, in a number of these countries–Japan is one example–household saving has declined recently. As we will see, a possibly more important source of the rise in the global supply of saving is the recent metamorphosis of the developing world from a net user to a net supplier of funds to international capital markets.

Table 1 provides a basis for a discussion of recent changes in global saving and financial flows by showing current account balances for different countries and regions, in billions of U.S. dollars, for the years 1996 (just before the U.S. current account deficit began to balloon) and 2003 (the most recent year for which complete data are available). I should note that these current account balances of necessity reflect realized patterns of investment and saving rather than changes in the rates of investment and saving desired from an *ex ante* perspective. Nevertheless, changes in the pattern of current account balances together with knowledge of changes in real interest rates should provide useful clues about shifts in the global supply of and demand for saving.

Table 1. Global Current Account Balances, 1996 and 2003 (Billions of U.S. dollars)

Countries	1996	2003
Industrial	46.2	-342.3
United States	-120.2	-530.7
Japan	65.4	138.2
Euro Area	88.5	24.9
France	20.8	4.5
Germany	-13.4	55.1
Italy	39.6	-20.7
Spain	0.4	-23.6
Other	12.5	25.3
Australia	-15.8	-30.4
Canada	3.4	17.1
Switzerland	21.3	42.2
United Kingdom	-10.9	-30.5
Developing	-87.5	205.0
Asia	-40.8	148.3
China	7.2	45.9
Hong Kong	-2.6	17.0
Korea	-23.1	11.9
Taiwan	10.9	29.3
Thailand	-14.4	8.0
Latin America	-39.1	3.8
Argentina	-6.8	7.4
Brazil	-23.2	4.0
Mexico	-2.5	-8.7
Middle East and Africa	5.9	47.8
E. Europe and the former Soviet Union	-13.5	5.1
Statistical discrepancy	41.3	137.2

The table confirms the sharp increase in the U.S. current account deficit, about $410 billion between 1996 and 2003. (Data from the first three quarters of 2004 imply that the current account deficit rose last year by an additional $140 billion at an annual rate.) In principle, the current account positions of the world's nations should sum to zero (although, in practice, data collection problems lead to a large statistical discrepancy, shown in the last row of table 1). The $410 billion increase in the U.S. current account deficit between 1996 and 2003 must therefore have been matched by a shift toward surplus of equal magnitude in other countries. Which countries experienced this change?

As we can infer from table 1, most of the swing toward surplus did not occur in the other industrial countries as a whole (although some individual industrial countries did experience large moves toward surplus, as we will see). The collective current account of the industrial countries declined more than $388 billion between 1996 and 2003, implying that, of the $410 billion increase in the U.S. current account deficit, only about $22 billion was offset by increased surpluses in other industrial countries. As table 1 shows, the bulk of the increase in the U.S. current account deficit was balanced by changes in the current account positions of developing countries, which moved from a collective deficit of $88 billion to a surplus of $205 billion–a net change of $293 billion–between 1996 and 2003.[7] The available data suggest that the current accounts of developing and emerging-market economies swung a further $60 billion into surplus in 2004.

This remarkable change in the current account balances of developing countries raises at least three questions. First, what events or factors induced this change? Second, what causal relationship (if any) exists between this change and current-account developments in the United States and in other industrial countries? Third, to the extent that the movement toward surplus in developing-country current accounts has had a differential impact on the United States relative to other industrial countries, what accounts for the difference?

In my view, a key reason for the change in the current account positions of developing countries is the series of financial crises those countries experienced in the past decade or so. In the mid-1990s, most developing countries were net importers of capital; as table 1 shows, in 1996 emerging Asia and Latin America borrowed about $80 billion on net on world capital markets. These capital inflows were not always productively used. In some cases, for example, developing-country governments borrowed to avoid necessary fiscal consolidation; in other cases, opaque and poorly governed banking systems failed to allocate those funds to the projects promising the highest returns. Loss of lender confidence, together with other factors such as overvalued fixed exchange rates and debt that was both short-term and denominated in foreign currencies, ultimately culminated in painful financial crises, including those in Mexico in 1994, in a number of East Asian countries in 1997-98, in Russia in 1998, in Brazil in 1999, and in Argentina in 2002. The effects of these crises included rapid capital outflows, currency depreciation, sharp declines in domestic asset prices, weakened banking systems, and recession.

In response to these crises, emerging-market nations either chose or were forced into new strategies for managing international capital flows. In general, these strategies involved shifting from being net importers of financial capital to being net exporters, in some cases very large net exporters. For example, in response to instability of capital flows and the exchange rate, some East Asian countries, such as Korea and Thailand, began to build up large quantities of foreign-exchange reserves and continued to do so even after the constraints imposed by the halt to capital inflows from global financial markets were relaxed. Increases in foreign-exchange reserves necessarily involve a shift toward surplus in the country's current account, increases in gross capital inflows, reductions in gross private capital outflows, or some combination of these elements. As table 1 shows, current account surpluses have been an important source of reserve accumulation in East Asia.

Countries in the region that had escaped the worst effects of the crisis but remained concerned about future crises, notably China, also built up reserves. These "war chests" of foreign reserves have been used as a buffer against potential capital outflows. Additionally, reserves were accumulated in the context of foreign exchange interventions intended to promote export-led growth by preventing exchange-rate appreciation. Countries typically pursue export-led growth because domestic demand is thought to be insufficient to employ fully domestic resources. Following the 1997-98 financial crisis, many of the East Asian countries seeking to stimulate their exports had high domestic rates of saving and, relative to historical norms, depressed levels of domestic capital investment–also consistent, of course, with strengthened current accounts.

In practice, these countries increased reserves through the expedient of issuing debt to their citizens, thereby mobilizing domestic saving, and then using the proceeds to buy U.S. Treasury securities and other assets. Effectively, governments have acted as financial intermediaries, channeling domestic saving away from local uses and into international capital markets. A related strategy has focused on reducing the burden of external debt by attempting to pay down those obligations, with the funds coming from a combination of reduced fiscal deficits and increased domestic debt issuance. Of necessity, this strategy also pushed emerging-market economies toward current account surpluses. Again, the shifts in current accounts in East Asia and Latin America are evident in the data for the regions and for individual countries shown in table 1.

Another factor that has contributed to the swing toward current-account surplus among the non-industrialized nations in the past few years is the sharp rise in oil prices. The current account surpluses of oil exporters, notably in the Middle East but also in countries such as Russia, Nigeria, and Venezuela, have risen as oil revenues have surged. For example, as table 1 shows, the collective current account surplus of the Middle East and Africa rose more than $40 billion between 1996 and 2003; it continued to swell in 2004 as oil prices increased yet further. In short, events since the mid-1990s have led to a large change in the collective current account position of the developing world, implying that many developing and emerging-market countries are now large net lenders rather than net borrowers on international financial markets.

Of course, developing countries as a group can increase their current account surpluses only if the industrial countries reduce their current accounts accordingly. How did this occur? Little evidence supports the view that the motivation to save has declined substantially in the industrial countries in recent years; indeed, as I have noted already, demographic factors should lead the industrial countries to try to save more, not less. Instead, the requisite shift in the collective external position of the industrial countries was facilitated by adjustments in asset prices and exchange rates, although the pattern of asset-price changes was somewhat different before and after 2000.

From about 1996 to early 2000, equity prices played a key equilibrating role in international financial markets. The development and adoption of new technologies and rising productivity in the United States–together with the country's long-standing advantages such as low political risk, strong property rights, and a good regulatory environment–made the U.S. economy exceptionally attractive to international investors during that period. Consequently, capital flowed rapidly into the United States, helping to fuel large appreciations in stock prices and in the value of the dollar. Stock indexes rose in other industrial countries as well, although stock-market capitalization per capita is significantly lower in those countries than in the United States.

The current account positions of the industrial countries adjusted endogenously to these changes in financial market conditions. I will focus here on the case of the United States, which bore the bulk of the adjustment. From the trade perspective, higher stock-market wealth increased the willingness of U.S. consumers to spend on goods and services, including large quantities of imports, while the strong dollar made U.S. imports cheap (in terms of dollars) and exports expensive (in terms of foreign currencies), creating a rising trade imbalance. From the saving-investment perspective, the U.S. current account deficit rose as capital investment increased (spurred by perceived profit opportunities) at the same time that the rapid increase in household wealth and expectations of future income gains reduced U.S. residents' perceived need to save. Thus the rapid increase in the U.S. current account deficit between 1996 and 2000 was fueled to a significant extent both by increased global saving and the greater interest on the part of foreigners in investing in the United States.

After the stock-market decline that began in March 2000, new capital investment and thus the demand for financing waned around the world. Yet desired global saving remained strong. The textbook analysis suggests that, with desired saving outstripping desired investment, the real rate of interest should fall to equilibrate the market for global saving. Indeed, real interest rates have been relatively low in recent years, not only in the United States but also abroad. From a narrow U.S. perspective, these low long-term rates are puzzling; from a global perspective, they may be less so.[8]

The weakening of new capital investment after the drop in equity prices did not much change the net effect of the global saving glut on the U.S. current account. The transmission mechanism changed, however, as low real interest rates rather than high stock prices became a principal cause of lower U.S. saving. In particular, during the past few years, the key asset-price effects of the global saving glut appear to have occurred in the market for residential investment, as low mortgage rates have supported record levels of home construction and strong gains in housing prices. Indeed, increases in home values, together with a stock-market recovery that began in 2003, have recently returned the wealth-to-income ratio of U.S. households to 5.4, not far from its peak value of 6.2 in 1999 and above its long-run (1960-2003) average of 4.8. The expansion of U.S. housing wealth, much of it easily accessible to households through cash-out refinancing and home equity lines of credit, has kept the U.S. national saving rate low–and indeed, together with the significant worsening of the federal budget outlook, helped to drive it lower. As U.S. business investment has recently begun a cyclical recovery while residential investment has remained strong, the domestic saving shortfall has continued to widen, implying a rise in the current account deficit and increasing dependence of the United States on capital inflows.[9]

According to the story I have sketched thus far, events outside U.S. borders–such as the financial crises that induced emerging-market countries to switch from being international borrowers to international lenders–have played an important role in the evolution of the U.S. current account deficit, with transmission occurring primarily through endogenous changes in equity values, house prices, real interest rates, and the exchange value of the dollar. One might ask why the current-account effects of the increase in desired global saving were felt disproportionately in the United States relative to other industrial countries. The attractiveness of the United States as an investment destination during the technology boom of the 1990s and the depth and sophistication of the country's financial markets (which, among other things, have allowed households easy access to housing wealth) have certainly been important. Another factor is the special international status of the U.S. dollar. Because the dollar is the leading international reserve currency, and because some emerging-market countries use the dollar as a reference point when managing the values of their own currencies, the saving flowing out of the developing world has been directed relatively more into dollar-denominated assets, such as U.S. Treasury securities. The effects of the saving outflow may thus have been felt disproportionately on U.S. interest rates and the dollar. For example, the dollar probably strengthened more in the latter 1990s than it would have if it had not been the principal reserve currency, enhancing the effect on the U.S. current account.

Most interesting, however, is that the experience of the United States in recent years is not so nearly unique among industrial countries as one might think initially. As shown in table 1, a number of key industrial countries other than the United States have seen their current accounts move substantially toward deficit since 1996, including France, Italy, Spain, Australia, and the United Kingdom. The principal exceptions to this trend among the major industrial countries are Germany and Japan, both of which saw substantial increases in their current account balances between 1996 and 2003 (and significant further increases in 2004). A key difference between the two groups of countries is that the countries whose current accounts have moved toward deficit have generally experienced substantial housing appreciation and increases in household wealth, while Germany and Japan–whose economies have been growing slowly despite very low interest rates–have not. For example, wealth-to-income ratios have risen since 1996 by 14 percent in France, 12 percent in Italy, and 27 percent in the United Kingdom; each of these countries has seen their current account move toward deficit, as already noted. By contrast, wealth-to-income ratios in Germany and Japan have remained flat.[10] The evident link between rising household wealth and a tendency for the current account to shift toward deficit is consistent with the mechanism that I have described today.

ECONOMIC AND POLICY IMPLICATIONS

I have presented today a somewhat unconventional explanation of the high and rising U.S. current account deficit. That explanation holds that one of the factors driving recent developments in the U.S. current account has been the very substantial shift in the current accounts of developing and emerging-market nations, a shift that has transformed these countries from net borrowers on international capital markets to large net lenders. This shift by developing nations, together with the high saving propensities of Germany, Japan, and some other major industrial nations, has resulted in a global saving glut. This increased supply of saving boosted U.S. equity values during the period of the stock market boom and helped to increase U.S. home values during the more recent period, as a consequence lowering U.S. national saving and contributing to the nation's rising current account deficit.

From a global perspective, are these developments economically beneficial or harmful? Certainly they have had some benefits. Most obviously, the developing and emerging-market countries that brought their current accounts into surplus did so to reduce their foreign debts, stabilize their currencies, and reduce the risk of financial crisis. Most countries have been largely successful in meeting each of these objectives. Thus, the shift of these economies from borrower to lender status has provided at least a short-term palliative for some of the problems they faced in the 1990s.

In the longer term, however, the current pattern of international capital flows–should it persist–could prove counterproductive. Most important, for the developing world to be lending large sums on net to the mature industrial economies is quite undesirable as a long-run proposition. Relative to their counterparts in the developing world, workers in industrial countries have large quantities of high-quality capital with which to work. Moreover, as I have already noted, the populations of most of these countries are both growing slowly and aging rapidly, implying that ratios of retirees to workers will rise sharply in coming decades. For example, in the United States, for every 100 people between the ages of 20 and 64, there are currently about 21 people aged 65 or older. According to United Nations projections, by 2030 the population of the United States will include about 34 people aged 65 or over for each 100 people in the 20-64 age range; for the Euro area and Japan, the analogous numbers in 2030 will be 46 and 57, respectively. Over the remainder of the century, the populations of other major industrial countries will age much more quickly than that of the United States. In 2050, for example, the number of retirees for each 100 working-age people in the United States should be about the same as in 2030, about 34, but the number of retirees per 100 working-age people is projected to increase to about 60 in the Euro area and about 78 in Japan.

We see that many of the major industrial countries–particularly Japan and some countries in Western Europe–have both strong reasons to save (to help support future retirees) and increasingly limited investment opportunities at home (because workforces are shrinking and capital-labor ratios are already high). In contrast, most developing countries have younger and more-rapidly growing workforces, as well as relatively low ratios of capital to labor, conditions that imply that the returns to capital in those countries may potentially be quite high.[11] Basic economic logic thus suggests that, in the longer term, the industrial countries as a group should be running current account surpluses and lending on net to the developing world, not the other way around. If financial capital were to flow in this "natural" direction, savers in the industrial countries would potentially earn higher returns and enjoy increased diversification, and borrowers in the developing world would have the funds to make the capital investments needed to promote growth and higher living standards. Of course, to ensure that capital flows to developing countries yield these benefits, the developing countries would need to make further progress toward improving conditions for investment, as I will discuss further in a bit.

A second issue concerns the uses of international credit in the United States and other industrial countries with external deficits. Because investment by businesses in equipment and structures has been relatively low in recent years (for cyclical and other reasons) and because the tax and financial systems in the United States and many other countries are designed to promote homeownership, much of the recent capital inflow into the developed world has shown up in higher rates of home construction and in higher home prices. Higher home prices in turn have encouraged households to increase their consumption. Of course, increased rates of homeownership and household consumption are both good things. However, in the long run, productivity gains are more likely to be driven by nonresidential investment, such as business purchases of new machines. The greater the extent to which capital inflows act to augment residential construction and especially current consumption spending, the greater the future economic burden of repaying the foreign debt is likely to be.

A third concern with the pattern of capital flows arises from the indirect effects of those flows on the sectoral composition of the economies that receive them. In the United States, for example, the growth in export-oriented sectors such as manufacturing has been restrained by the U.S. trade imbalance (although the recent decline in the dollar has alleviated that pressure somewhat), while sectors producing nontraded goods and services, such as home construction, have grown rapidly. To repay foreign creditors, as it must someday, the United States will need large and healthy export industries. The relative shrinkage in those industries in the presence of current account deficits–a shrinkage that may well have to be reversed in the future–imposes real costs of adjustment on firms and workers in those industries.

Finally, the large current account deficit of the United States, in particular, requires substantial flows of foreign financing. As I have discussed today, the underlying sources of the U.S. current account deficit appear to be medium-term or even long-term in nature, suggesting that the situation will eventually begin to improve, although a return to approximate balance may take some time. Fundamentally, I see no reason why the whole process should not proceed smoothly. However, the risk of a disorderly adjustment in financial markets always exists, and the appropriately conservative approach for policymakers is to be on guard for any such developments.

What policy options exist to deal with the U.S. current account deficit? I have downplayed the role of the U.S. federal budget deficit today, and I disagree with the view, sometimes heard, that balancing the federal budget *by itself* would largely defuse the current account issue. In particular, to the extent that a reduction in the federal budget resulted in lower interest rates, the principal effects might be increased consumption and investment spending at home rather than a lower current account deficit. Indeed, a recent study suggests that a one-dollar reduction in the federal budget deficit would cause the current account deficit to decline less than 20 cents (Erceg, Guerrieri, and Gust, 2005). These results imply that even if we could balance the federal budget tomorrow, the medium-term effect would likely be to reduce the current account deficit by less than one percentage point of GDP.

Although I do not believe that plausible near-term changes in the federal budget would eliminate the current account deficit, I should stress that reducing the federal budget deficit is still a good idea. Although the effects on the current account of reining in the budget deficit would likely be relatively modest, at least the direction is right. Moreover, there are other good reasons to bring down the federal budget deficit, including the reduction of the debt obligations that will have to be serviced by taxpayers in the future. Similar observations apply to policy recommendations to increase household saving in the United States, for example by creating tax-favored saving vehicles. Although the effect of saving-friendly policies on the U.S. current account deficit might not be dramatic, again the direction would be right. Moreover, increasing U.S. national saving from its current low level would support productivity and wealth creation and help our society make better provision for the future.

However, as I have argued today, some of the key reasons for the large U.S. current account deficit are external to the United States, implying that purely inward-looking policies are unlikely to resolve this issue. Thus a more direct approach is to help and encourage developing countries to re-enter international capital markets in their more natural role as borrowers, rather than as lenders. For example, developing countries could improve their investment climates by continuing to increase macroeconomic stability, strengthen property rights, reduce corruption, and remove barriers to the free flow of financial capital. Providing assistance to developing countries in strengthening their financial institutions–for example, by improving bank regulation and supervision and by increasing financial transparency–could lessen the risk of financial crises and thus increase both the willingness of those countries to accept capital inflows and the willingness of foreigners to invest there. Financial liberalization is a particularly attractive option, as it would help both to permit capital inflows to find the highest-return uses and, by easing borrowing constraints, to spur domestic consumption. Other changes will occur naturally over time. For example, the pace at which emerging-market countries are accumulating international reserves should slow as they increasingly perceive their reserves to be adequate and as they move toward more flexible exchange rates. The factors underlying the U.S. current account deficit are likely to unwind only gradually, however. Thus, we probably have little choice except to be patient as we work to create the conditions in which a greater share of global saving can be redirected away from the United States and toward the rest of the world–particularly the developing nations.

REFERENCES

Erceg, Christopher, Luca Guerrieri, and Christopher Gust (2005)."Expansionary Fiscal Shocks and the Trade Deficit." International

Finance Discussion Paper 2005-825. Washington: Board of Governors of the Federal Reserve System (January).

Greenspan, Alan (2005). "Current account." Speech at Advancing Enterprise 2005 Conference, London, February 4.

End Notes

[1] As U.S. capital outflows in those three quarters totaled $728 billion at an annual rate, gross financing needs exceeded $1.3 trillion.

[2] I thank David Bowman, Joseph Gagnon, Linda Kole, and Maria Perozek of the Board staff for excellent assistance.

[3] For simplicity, I will use the term "net foreign borrowing" to refer to the financing of the current account deficit, though strictly speaking this financing involves the sale of foreign and domestic assets as well as the issuance of debt securities to foreigners. As illustrated by the data in footnote 1, U.S. gross foreign borrowing is much larger than net foreign borrowing, as gross borrowing must be sufficient to offset not only the deficit in current payments but also U.S. capital outflows.

[4] This definition of capital investment ignores many less tangible forms of investment, such as research and development expenditures. It also ignores investment in human capital, such as educational expenses. Using a more inclusive definition of investment could well change our perceptions of U.S. saving and investment trends quite substantially. I will leave that topic for another day.

[5] The Bureau of Economic Analysis treats government investment–in roads or schools, for instance–as part of national saving in the national income accounts. Thus, strictly speaking, national saving is reduced by the government deficit net of government investment, not by the entire government deficit. The difference between domestic investment and national saving is not affected by this qualification, however, as government investment and the implied adjustment to national saving cancel each other out.

[6] By "high desired saving" I mean a supply schedule for saving that is shifted far to the right. Actual or realized saving depends on the equilibrium values of the real interest rate and other economic variables.

[7] The statistical discrepancy also increased substantially, by $96 billion on net. As asset accumulation in developing countries may be less completely measured than in industrial countries, a significant part of the change in the discrepancy may represent an additional movement toward surplus in developing-country current accounts.

[8] In pointing out the possible effects of strong global saving on real interest rates, I do not mean to rule out other factors. For example, a lowering of risk premiums resulting from increased macroeconomic and monetary stability has likely played some role.

[9] Greenspan (2005) notes a strong correlation between U.S. mortgage debt and the U.S. current account deficit.

[10] These data are from Annex Table 58, OECD Economic Outlook, vol. 76, 2004, p. 226. The latest year for which data are available is 2003 for Germany and the United Kingdom, 2002 for France, Italy, and Japan.

[11] China is an important exception to the generalization that developing countries have young populations. The country's fertility rate has declined since the 1970s, and its elderly dependency ratio is expected to exceed that of the United States by midcentury.

INDEX

A

B

C

D

E

F

G

H

V

W

Y